# Splashes of Joy in the Cesspools of Life

# BARBARA JOHNSON

WORD PUBLISHING
Dallas·London·Vancouver·Melbourne

SPLASHES OF JOY IN THE CESSPOOLS OF LIFE

Scripture quotations used in this book are from the following sources:

The King James Version of the Bible (KJV).

The Holy Bible, New International Version (NIV). Copyright © 1973, 1978, 1984 International Bible Society. Used by permission of Zondervan Bible Publishers.

The New King James Version (NKJV). Copyright © 1979, 1980, 1982, Thomas Nelson, Inc., Publisher.

The Revised Standard Version of the Bible (RSV), copyrighted 1946, 1952, © 1971, 1973 by the Division of Christian Education of the National Council of the Churches of Christ in the U.S.A. Used by permission.

*The Living Bible* (TLB). Copyright © 1971 by Tyndale House Publishers, Wheaton, Illinois. Used by permission.

The Holy Bible, New Century Version (NCV). Copyright © 1987, 1988, 1991 by Word Publishing, Dallas, Texas 75039. Used by permission.

p. cm.
ISBN 0–8499–3313–7

*Printed in the United States of America*

This book is dedicated to my OLDER and THINNER sister, Janet, who has fondly called me "Punk" for as long as I can remember. Her best quality is her tender heart. When our kids were small, Janet and I took them to see the movie *The Adventures of Tom Sawyer* at a drive-in theater. It was much too violent for her. When Tom's Aunt Polly thumped him on the head with her thimble for being mischievous, Janet made us leave. But she has always been there for me, as she has for so many others. She cries easily (but always appropriately), and she will surely cry when she reads this excerpt from Carey Martin's essay, "What Is a Sister?" which is especially true for her:

A sister is one of the most precious people in the story of your life. Together, you have shared some of the most special moments two people have ever shared. A sister is a perspective on the past, and she's a million favorite memories that will always last. A sister is a photograph that is one of your most treasured possessions. She's a note that arrives on a special day, and when there's news to share, she's the first one you want to call. A sister is a reminder of the blessings that come from closeness.

A sister is a confidante and a counselor. She's a dear and wonderful friend, and—in certain ways—something like a twin. She's a hand within your hand; she's so often the only one who understands.

What is a sister? She's someone more special than words; someone beautiful and unique. And in so many ways, there is no one who is loved so dearly.

# *Contents*

# Acknowledgments

I gratefully extend appreciation and thanks to the many people who have so graciously shared with me the stories, poems, letters, and other materials that appear in this book. You have provided some of the biggest splashes of joy in my life!

Diligent effort has been made to locate the author and copyright ownership of all material quoted in this book. However, because I receive clippings, handwritten notes, church bulletins, etc., from friends and readers all over the world, there often is no way of identifying the original source. Many of the anecdotes and tidbits used in this book are combinations of materials from different sources, and the letters I share have been changed and/or combined so that the writers' identities are protected. If any readers know the correct source of the items now designated as "Source unknown," I would appreciate hearing from you so corrections can be made in later printings and proper credit can be given.

Special acknowledgment and my sincere thanks also go to the following individuals and companies for these materials:

Ashleigh Brilliant for permission to use Ashleigh Brilliant *Pot-Shots* and *Brilliant Thoughts* (Brilliant Enterprises, 117 West Valerio St., Santa Barbara, California 93101).

The Russ Postcard cartoon feature by Dana Summers, included in chapter 1. Used by permission.

# Introduction
## "Barb, I Need a Splash of Your Joy . . ."

Not long ago I paid a visit to Focus on the Family to tape a radio interview with Dr. James Dobson, the founder and president. While we sat in his office, sharing our latest experiences, I sensed that he wasn't in his usual "up" kind of mood. There was a definite heaviness in his voice that wasn't typical of him.

I knew Dr. Dobson had been serving on the Attorney General's Commission on Pornography and that for over a year he had been spending one week every month traveling to various cities throughout the United States to study the problem. He had even received threatening letters and phone calls for taking part in the program, and it was obvious that all those months of stress had been a drain on him, physically as well as emotionally.

Sensing Dr. Dobson's downcast mood, I offered to come back at another time. "Then we could do the interview when you are feeling more refreshed and ready to go . . . ," I suggested.

Dr. Dobson just looked at me and said, "Barb, if there EVER were a time that I needed a splash of your joy, it's today!"

We went ahead with the interview and it came out much better than any of us had hoped. Later, I thought about what he had said.

Someday, I told myself, I'd like to write a book that would have refreshing words that could help others find "splashes of joy," no matter what situation they find themselves in. So, in a way, I owe part of the title for this book to Dr. Dobson, who tossed off that phrase, "splash of joy" so easily, never thinking it would become part of a book designed to inject some joy and hope into a joyless, hopeless world.

So now you know where the first part of the title came from, but what about the rest of it? Some of my friends told me that using a word like "cesspools" in a title would sound too graphic, and I listened carefully to what they were saying. But the more I continued to hear from folks out there who are in pain of every imaginable description, the more I realized that that's exactly where they are—in one kind of slimy cesspool or another.

Most of us can think about times when we've been "in the cesspool"; many of you are there right now. Almost everyone needs a splash of joy to get through the mess, to get cleaned off and get sweetened up—refreshed and ready to go again.

For several years I used the phrase "In His Grip" when autographing books requested at conferences or by mail. But to be honest, that got tiresome because of having to go back and dot all those *i*'s. Since I sign hundreds of books, I decided I wanted something that would be meaningful, but without so many places where I would have to dot some *i*'s or cross some *t*'s.

Finally, I came upon the perfect word. JOYFULLY says it all. In JOYFULLY there is nothing to dot or cross—it just flows out. It's a word that is a little "splash of joy" for me because it gives me the perfect trademark for every book that I autograph. JOYFULLY simply means "full of joy." What a blessing to have found one little word that I can make my own. It says what I feel, simply and completely, and it is the key to the way I live my life.

That's what this book is all about—living life joyfully. I want to bring you splashes of joy, whether you feel you're in a slimy cesspool or just a dirty mudhole that is causing you stress and frustration. Because of my books and Spatula Ministries, I get a lot of feedback that turns into splashes of joy for me. One dear woman wrote this darling note:

*God uses you like an antiseptic on wounds to bring healing to the Body of Christ.—*

*Thanks* ♡

Another good friend wrote to say that so many people are hoping to hear words of encouragement as they ". . . search for a way out of the tunnel of despair, the slough of despond, the quagmire of panic, the quicksand of hopelessness . . . and all those kinds of places. God is using you to help people through."

Letters like that give back to me splashes of joy, as do comments made by women after they hear me as a retreat speaker. We gather in a circle after I spend three days telling them everything I know (actually, it takes less than three days, but I repeat myself a lot). Then I offer them the opportunity to talk about how they feel. Almost everyone shares and can hardly wait to get her turn. Those are times when the splashes of joy become little tidal waves that wash over me as I am reminded of Proverbs 11:25— as you refresh others, you, yourself, will be refreshed.

So I guess I'm writing this book for myself as much as for you. We both need splashes of joy, so let's go find some!

Joyfully,

*Barbara Johnson*

# Smile! It Kills Time Between Disasters

*Life is what you make it,*
*until something comes along and makes it worse.*

When I opened the package, I should have known that THESE pantyhose would be "different." But somehow I just didn't get suspicious, even when they came wrapped as a gift just before April Fools' Day, given to me by a friend who was working in the novelty shop at Knott's Berry Farm. When I took them out of the box, they looked like any other pantyhose and I thought, *How nice of Alice to send these. I can always use another pair.*

Just two days later—on April 1—I decided to wear the new pantyhose while speaking nearby to a large group of women at a church brunch. When I pulled on the pantyhose that morning, I guess I should have realized something was a bit strange because they came clear up to my ARMPITS! Bill even commented, "What have you got on? It looks like a SA-RONG!"

I just ignored my "tell-it-like-it-is" husband and hurriedly finished dressing. *Obviously, Alice bought the wrong size, I told myself, but there's nothing to be done about it now because I don't have time to change . . . I've got to be at the church in twenty minutes . . .*

The program went nicely, but as I got up to speak, I felt something beginning to creep up on me. I had on a V-neck dress and, looking down, I was horrified to see something brown inching its way right up out of my neckline! The brown stuff just kept coming, and soon it seemed to be like some kind of muff around my throat. Then I realized what was going on. Those pantyhose Alice had given me were made of material that *really* stretched. (I learned later they were 100 percent SPANDEX!) My new pantyhose had actually begun to "grow north"—straight up over my head! I could have tied them at the top in a bow!

What to do? There was no way to shove the pantyhose down my dress without making a big bulge in the wrong place. Besides, I was in front of five hundred women, with no privacy to do anything. I decided to stop and tell the crowd that I had a friend who knows I love the first of each month—especially April Fools' Day. She must have thought it would be great fun to give me a pair of "unique" pantyhose—the kind that could creep up clear around my neck!

Once the women understood that my problem was my pantyhose and not some strange growth caused by spores from outer space, they all began laughing and enjoying my embarrassment along with me. Not many speakers get to finish a presentation with a brown muff that appears magically from out of their dress. It was a first for my audience, and it was DEFINITELY a first for me. But we all had a good time because I chose not to get flustered. Instead, I enjoyed making the best of the situation.

When you look at all the pain and problems in the world, creeping pantyhose isn't exactly a 7.2 on the Richter scale of human suffering. It does, however, illustrate the fact that there is something about joy and laughter that is engaging and even therapeutic, especially when things aren't going very well. The overwhelming response to a recent book I did—*So, Stick a Geranium in Your Hat and Be Happy*—is hard to explain, unless you

take into account the tremendous need so many folks have for some kind of relief, something to bring a smile or chuckle into a life that, as one letter said, "doesn't have any sparkles right now."

The following paragraphs offer just a peek into my post office box, which is the landing place for up to several dozen letters a day, almost always from women who are in, or just crawled out of, one of the slippery cesspools of life. Pain has MANY faces, and the universal cure is laughter—not because we try to deny the truth, but because we have learned to face it, absorb it, and smile through it.

From New York:

How I wish I could meet you face to face and speak with you. Sometimes I feel like no one understands my pain. My husband and I also lost two children. Donna, a beautiful young lady, turned to a life of prostitution and in November '84 she was murdered at the age of 22. We never did see her in her coffin—they shipped her home sealed.

A few months later, Jerry, age 27 contracted AIDS because of his gay lifestyle, and at age 28 he went home to be with

Jesus. . . . When our children died, everyone kept telling us to rejoice. We tried to, and in the interim I denied the reality of my grief and now I'm unable to cry, so the only emotion that comes from me is anger . . . I am so uptight right now I feel like a pressure cooker about to explode. I spend a lot of time with the Lord in prayer . . . the only time I get any relief from my terrible anxiety. . . .

Please pray for me. I'm a mess who's waiting for God to make something beautiful. He truly is the Rock that is higher than myself, and I continually run to Him, sometimes pleading for strength to make it through the next moment. . . .

## From Colorado:

I found out last week that my son is HIV positive and has been ill a lot this winter. He called last Sunday night. Only God knows my pain and my son's fright.

Today I don't feel like I can hang on to God, so I'm letting God hang on to me, my son and my husband. . . .

## From California:

It was just one year ago that our daughter had her diving accident and went to be with the Lord. We still miss her so much, but knowing where she is makes it easier to bear. . . .

## From Alabama:

My life fell apart four years ago. We had a wonderful life, prosperous, one son, one daughter, beautiful home, health, etc. Our daughter announced her lesbianism at the start of her senior year in school.

Nine months later, my husband left me and our son without one word of warning (after 22 years together). I found out he was having an affair with a woman at his job. . . .

But my faith in God has never been stronger . . . and I still have my sense of humor! I know that God is in control, even though my life seems to be so out of control.

## From Oregon:

It is Christmas morning with all the snow and the wonderful music of this happy season. I have just finished reading your book for the umpteenth time and as I type this I am smiling.

I do not smile often, but I am learning to laugh again. You see, my sister, Jean, died of cancer, my dear, dear husband shot himself in our bedroom, my father died of cancer, I lost my job after several years and then in July of last year I was rear-ended in an auto accident. I still cannot work full time, but I have gone back to school.

In the middle of the night I wake up with such desolation, fear, and the purely personal feeling of WHY? In the midst of all this I think I have truly found God again. I also know in my heart He has wonderful things planned for me. I just must find the faith to wait until He is ready to show me the path that I must follow.

## From Nevada:

A year ago I lost my 21-year-old son by suicide. It has been a truly lost year for me and my family. A friend recently sent me a copy of your book, *Stick a Geranium in Your Hat and Be Happy*. The book helped me in many ways. I wanted you to know. I think it will also help some of the members of my support group.

## From Missouri·

While I have not experienced any of your devastating losses and heartaches, I've had my own—my divorce after 19 years of what I thought was a good marriage; my oldest daughter living with her boyfriend, marrying him, and now, after four and a half years, facing divorce; my other daughter becoming pregnant at 17, getting married, having a beautiful baby boy, getting divorced, and remarried all in less that a year's time. But the beauty of it all was that God was with me through each experience. He not only shared my burdens, but sent others to help share the burdens and pain, too.

PAIN IS INEVITABLE BUT MISERY IS OPTIONAL!!! Thanks again.

## How to Find Joy in the Midst of It All

These excerpts from my mail are just the tip of an iceberg infinitely bigger than the one that sank the Titanic. I have enough letters like this to fill this book—and several more like it. Thousands of us want to know how to find some splashes of joy—and, eventually, how to climb out of the cesspool and back to happier places.

I've been there in the dark, dank, lonely cesspool, and somehow—with God's loving help—I have managed to climb out. Still, seldom a day goes by that I'm not reminded of that cesspool; sometimes, I find myself teetering on the edge, ready to slide back in again. I don't have any magic pills or formulas, but FINDING JOY IN THE MIDST OF MISERY always works for me, and I know it can work for you, too.

## Rubbish Removal for the Mind

Over the years I have learned some strategies for finding splashes of joy when life turns into a cesspool. Actually, *strategies* is not quite the right word. I leave the technical stuff to my husband, Bill, the engineer in the family. I prefer to share my *ways to live*—simple things that work for me, and they are all tied to one of my favorite verses:

> Fix your thoughts on what is true and good and right.
>     Think about things that are pure and lovely,
> And dwell on the fine, good things in others.
>     Think about all you can praise God for
>         And be glad about it.
>                     Philippians 4:8, TLB

I call Philippians 4:8 my "rubbish removal service." It's the verse I use to dump the garbage from my mind and get rid of useless, rotting, noxious junk so I can replace it with things that are nourishing, fresh, and healthy. A lot has been written on "positive thinking," but Paul scooped everybody two thousand years ago with Philippians 4:8, which he wrote in prison, chained to a Roman guard, waiting to be executed.

In a JOY-*LESS* place, in JOY-*LESS* circumstances, Paul was JOY-*FULL* because he knew that the difference between splashes of joy and the cesspool often depends on how you want to look at what is happening to you and around you.

Not long ago I began noticing how the household products I use suggest the importance of one's attitude. For example, I like to use FRESH START laundry soap because it reminds me that Christians can have a fresh start. First John 1:9 promises us that if we confess our sins we are cleansed from all unrighteousness. That means that the past is a canceled check, tomorrow is a promissory note, and today is CASH. "Thank You, Lord," I pray in the morning, "for a new day that isn't even messed up yet—a fresh start. Thank you for a whole day full of exciting things . . . new experiences . . . new challenges."

I also use JOY detergent on my dishes, and while I appreciate the "lemon-fresh smell," I like the idea of finding joy in new beginnings even better. Joy is the land of beginning again for every Christian. Joy is having God live in the marrow of your bones. Happiness depends on what is going on around us, but joy bubbles up from deep within because of what God does for us. Happiness is elusive and can be wiped out in a second, but abiding joy from the Lord is like a deep river down in your heart that just keeps flowing.

Thinking about those two products helped me so much I started collecting more and more names, like ZEST, CHEER, GLAD, and PRAISE, to name just a few of several dozens that I have found. Then, just for fun, a friend of mine put them together in a little imaginary story which I have started sharing at conferences and seminars. It goes like this:

### An Opera Full of Soap
### (and Other Things)

As a young Christian mother, I loved living my life in mental IVORY palaces. It was NEVER DULL as I sought to raise my children with INTENSIVE CARE because I always had my godly husband to CARESS at night.

My Christian life was full of ZEST. There was so much to PRAISE God for. My own walk with the Lord started when I saw the DAWN, confessed my sins, and they VANISHed. I stood FAULTLESS before the Lord. Another JOY was that my children had PLEDGEd their lives to Christ. A final PERK was that my husband seemed to have a BOLD witness for the Lord. I thought I'd live like this until I went to GLORY, but lo and BEHOLD the TIDE turned.

First, my husband, who had been MR. CLEAN to me, said he needed a change and WISKed himself off with another woman. This was no BREEZE to me. Then a week later my middle son DIALed me on the phone and told me he was gay. All I could do was SHOUT.

I DASHed to my church for help, but my SOS call did nothing for my hurt PRIDE, and I fell into a depression. I began to GAIN a lot of weight. I was in such a pit that I stopped going to church and completely lost my SPARKLE.

Then an old friend called me. She was as good as GOLD. I told her my life was no JUBILEE. She said it didn't matter, and that her life wasn't SPIC AND SPAN, either. She said that if we shared together and put on the SHIELD of faith, we could get a FRESH START. We did—we prayed and talked together and got the spiritual SOFTSCRUB on the inside until we felt KLEAN 'N' SHINEd. My eyes began to have a TWINKLE again.

I'm GLAD my life worked out as it did because I've learned to live in a CLING FREE sort of way. I don't expect my family to be PERFECT for my own happiness. Sometimes I fail and my mind gets EZily OFF the track, but then I pray and the Holy Spirit comes in and RENUZIT. I anticipate that blessed LIFT-OFF when Jesus comes to take me to GLORY. Until then, I'm going to SNUGGLE up to the Word, and serve God.

The best part of my little household-products tale concerns putting on the SHIELD of faith and getting a FRESH START by SNUGGLE-ing up to the Word and serving God. I heard somewhere that the average woman spends fourteen years of her life doing household chores. Her husband may retire, but the typical woman keeps right on working—scrubbing, polishing, and using many of the products mentioned above. I started thinking about how we spend all that time cleaning and wondered if there wouldn't be some way to make the time more productive. What can we do with those fourteen years we're spending with our hands in the sink, our heads in the toilet, and our minds who knows where? Surely there has to be a way to get our minds off grime, rust, and stains and center it on what is good, pure, and lovely.

## Scripture Memorization Made Easy

One of the best approaches to making household chores more inspiring comes from my daughter-in-love, Shannon, who is married to my son, Barney. She types out Bible verses that apply to the name of the product she is using (for example, verses on JOY) and then tapes them right on the back of the bottle. When she uses GLORY floor wax, she types out verses on glory and tapes them on the back of the container. She does this with all kinds of products, then she memorizes the verses as she does her household chores. When these verses are committed to memory, she peels them off the various containers and replaces them with more verses that apply to that same product.

It is amazing how many Scriptures come to mind when you think about words like PRAISE, SHOUT, BEHOLD, etc. Sometimes the verses seem to jump right out at you, and before you realize it you are bringing your thoughts into captivity, as it says in 2 Corinthians 10:5.

How much we need the balance and control that a reservoir of Scripture can bring into our lives! I used to sing a little chorus in Sunday school: "Thy word have I hid in my heart that I might not sin against Thee . . . that I might not sin . . . that I might not sin . . . that I might not sin against Thee." I learned that little song when I was about six years old, and those words (from Ps. 119:11) are still clearly imprinted in my memory.

When I was growing up, a little cardboard plaque hung in our dining room. It had blue and gold letters that said, "Let the words of my mouth, and the meditation of my heart, be acceptable in thy sight, O LORD, my strength, and my redeemer" (Ps. 19:14, KJV). That plaque is a frozen frame in my video of memories, and I can still see the words, which are part of my reservoir of Scripture.

We know that Scripture SHOULD be put to memory, but getting time to do it is something else. Putting verses on the backs of household products is a simple, easy way to make your chores less boring, and at the same time you are filling your mind with edifying thoughts from God, Himself. It works for Shannon and it works for me. I now make it a habit to be on the lookout for verses that are brought to mind by products I use.

For example, while walking through a local department store this week, I passed the cosmetic counter and saw a jar of face cream called ETERNAL and immediately John 3:16 came to mind. Right next to that were perfumes called PROMISE and REMEMBRANCE. Automatically, I began thinking of verses that would go with these fragrances. Second Peter 1:4 talks about God's "great and precious promises" (NIV) through which we can escape the world's corruption. There are many promises in Scripture, and you can pick the ones you like the best. One of my favorites is Romans 8:28, and I also like Psalm 34:19 (NIV): "A righteous man may have many troubles, but the LORD delivers him from them all."

As for REMEMBRANCE, it suggests many wonderful passages, particularly Christ's words at the first communion, "This is my body, given for you; do this in remembrance of Me" (Luke 22:19, NIV). And in John 14:26, Jesus talked about the Holy Spirit, how He would teach His disciples all things and "bring to your remembrance all things that I said to you" (NKJV).

After seeing a product called PROMISE at a cosmetic counter, I was reminded that PROMISE is also the name of a margarine. So, whether you're in a department store or in a super-market, all kinds of name brands can jump out to remind you to fix your thoughts on what is true, good, right, and lovely. What better way to do that than to commit the Word of God to memory as you clean, scrub, and shop?

## Every Morning You Have a Choice

How we use the time God gives us is our choice every day. We can live as though Christ died yesterday, rose today, and is coming tomorrow, or we can live as though Christ died, pe-riod. We can count blessings, or we can count calamities. We can count blessings, or we can count life's blows and burdens. It's our choice.

All the FANTASTIC household products that make life so much easier today remind me of some instructions an Appala-chian grandmother gave a new bride years ago concerning how to wash clothes. You might want to copy it and stick it up over your automatic washer and dryer. Then, every time you're tempted to have a pity party because life isn't so perfect, you can read it and remember that life is *always a choice*.

WASHDAY, 1916

1. Bild fire in backyard to heet kettle of rain water.
2. Set tubs so smoke won't blow in eyes if wind is pert.
3. Shave one hold cake lie soap in bilin water.
4. Sort things, make three piles, 1 pile white, 1 pile colored, 1 pile work britches and rags.
5. Stir flour in cold water to smooth, then thin down with bilin water.
6. Rub dirty spots on board, scrub hard, then bile. Rub col-ored, don't bile, just rinch in starch.
7. Take white things out of kettle with broomstick handle, then rinch and starch.
8. Hang old rags on fince.
9. Spread tee towels on grass.
10. Pore rinch water in flower bed.

11. Scrub porch with hot soapy water.
12. Turn tubs upside down.
13. Go put on fresh dress, smooth hair with side combs, brew cup of tea, sit and rest and rock a spell, and count blessings.

I like her advice. What I get out of her words is that you have to make some choices before the blessings are there to count. The following poem is from a Wichita, Kansas, church newsletter. I have no idea who wrote it, but whoever did understood the power of attitude.

We Choose . . .

We choose how we shall live;
courageously or in cowardice,
honorably or dishonorably,
with purpose or in drift.
We decide what is important
and what is trivial in life.
We decide that what makes us significant
is either what we do or refuse to do . . .
WE DECIDE.
WE CHOOSE.
And as we decide and as we choose,
so our lives are formed . . .

"But, Barb," people ask me, "how can I make the choice to be positive when life is so negative?" Remember Philippians 4:8. You will be joyful if you want to think that way. Or you will be sad and depressed if you so choose. As someone said:

AN OPTIMIST LOOKS AT AN OYSTER
AND EXPECTS TO FIND A PEARL.
A PESSIMIST LOOKS AT AN OYSTER
AND EXPECTS PTOMAINE POISONING.

Pessimism seems to be in fashion lately. With all the bad news that you can tune in any time between 4:00 and 11:00 P.M., people may think you've gone "Looney Tunes" if you're optimistic. The truth, however, according to some psychologists, is that optimism is a much more effective way to live. One of the best uses of optimism is for fighting depression, that overwhelming feeling of helplessness or hopelessness that you get when you experience a loss, a failure, or a heavy disappointment. I love the bumper "snicker" that says:

> A PESSIMIST IS SOMEONE WHO FEELS BAD
> WHEN SHE FEELS GOOD
> FOR FEAR SHE WILL FEEL WORSE
> WHEN SHE FEELS BETTER.

On the other hand, optimism helps turn life around. The experts say that optimistic people achieve more in life, enjoy better health, age more comfortably, and live longer than pessimists. I like that, especially the part about "aging more comfortably."[1]

## Set Your Automatic Pilot on "Optimistic"

It's good to hear that a pessimist can learn to be an optimist (I've been trying to tell Bill that for years). The best way to start learning to be an optimist is to change the way you think, especially how you explain to yourself the reasons why things happen and why life unfolds the way it does.

Pessimists tend to think negatively without realizing it. It's almost as if they are on some kind of negative automatic pilot. One example I love to use is the difference in how Bill and I look at things—even the weather. On one of the rare, smog-free, glorious days we have in Southern California, I looked up at the azure blue sky and the fleecy white clouds and said, "Wow, it looks as if God vacuumed the sky."

Bill looked up at the same sky and said, "Yeah, but He'll probably dump the vacuum bag tomorrow."

To put all that another way, an optimist would invent the airplane. If Bill had his choice, he would invent the parachute.

You see, the pessimist thinks he's taking a chance while the optimist feels he is grasping a great opportunity. If you are the type who might be looking for rain when there isn't a cloud in the sky, try to *become alert to your automatic thoughts.* Start being aware of the negative things you say about yourself, others, and life. When you realize you're talking negatively, just tell yourself to STOP. Set your mind's automatic pilot on "optimistic," and repeat Philippians 4:8 as a prayer—something like this:

> Lord, whenever I hear or read rumors, gossip, or just plain lies, help me fix my thoughts on what is true, good, and right. Help me tune out what is negative and suggestive and tune in what is pure and lovely.
>
> When I get irritated with others and start finding fault, help me dwell on the fine things in them. Help me forget about their faults and remember their strengths.
>
> And when I start feeling sorry for myself, help me remember all the reasons why I should praise You. Remind me of all the blessings You bring into my life to make me happy.

## Smile—It Increases Your Face Value

Smiles are everywhere if you just take the trouble to look. There can even be a smile in how a book title gets garbled in a person's mind. I've had a lot of good examples of that with my last book (I call it *Geranium* for short). For instance, a woman from California who heard me on the radio got the title wrong *twice* in the same letter:

> I enjoyed the program you graced with your gift of gab. I don't read books but I might enjoy "Feather in My Hat" or whatever. I need a laugh in life and I know a few other people can say the same. . . .
>
> Hope you don't mind my long note just to order your book. I called the station and was advised "Flower in My Hat" would be an uplift.

As far as I'm concerned, it doesn't matter—feathers, flowers, or geraniums—just so I can give folks like this an uplift.

One of my favorite optimistic poems is this:

> Life is easier than you think.
>   All you have to do is:
>   Accept the impossible,
> Do without the indispensable,
>   Bear the intolerable,
>     and
> Be able to smile at anything.
>
>     Source unknown

To be able to "smile at anything"—that's the key. Not only does smiling kill time between disasters, but it also helps your attitude, and we all have to work hard to avoid hardening of the attitudes!

Dr. Charles Swindoll, pastor of the Evangelical Free Church of Fullerton, California, is one of the most optimistic, "up" people I have ever met. He always has a smile and loves to laugh. He is a living, breathing example of the power of attitude. He writes:

> The longer I live, the more I realize the impact of attitude on life. Attitude, to me, is more important than facts. It is more important than the past, than education, than money, than circumstances, than failures, than successes, than what other people think or say or do. It is more important than appearance, giftedness, or skill. It will make or break a company . . . a church . . . a home. The remarkable thing is we have a choice every day regarding the attitude we will embrace for that day. We cannot change our past . . . we cannot change the fact that people will act in a certain way. We cannot change the inevitable. The only thing we can do is play on the one string we have, and that is our attitude. . . .[2]

Play on your one string as optimistically as you can. Make the best of it, even when you get the worst of it—and never forget that every day holds the possibility of miracles. As an unknown poet said:

### FRESH NEW DAY

If you awake and see the sunrise
Bathing earth in red and gold,
As you gaze you'll somehow find
It brings a washing of the soul.
It fills one with anticipation
To start the day with such a sight.
God is so very good to give
A fresh new day, giftwrapped so bright!

Source unknown

## Splish/Splash . . .

OPTIMISM IS HAVING THREE TEEN-AGE SONS
AND ONLY ONE CAR.

\*    \*    \*    \*    \*    \*

### VALUES

So often folks have wondered why
    God has placed on earth
The storms, the tears, the raging seas—
    Destroyers of all worth.
But if it weren't for angry skies,
    The torrents, and dismay,
How could we realize the worth
    Of a sunny, cloudless day?

Source unknown

\*    \*    \*    \*    \*    \*

A PESSIMIST HAS NO STARTER,
AN OPTIMIST HAS NO BRAKES.

\*    \*    \*    \*    \*    \*

IN THE LONG RUN, PESSIMISTS MAY BE PROVEN RIGHT,
BUT THE OPTIMIST HAS A BETTER TIME ON THE TRIP.

\* \* \* \* \* \*

### CHEERY-O!

If you smile the day will be cheery,
   If you smile the day will be bright.
If you think good thoughts you'll be happy,
   And everything will work out just right.
So don't let a frown turn you sour,
   Don't let bad thoughts make you blue.
Just always remember, think positively,
   For how you feel is up to you!

                 Susan L. Wiener

\* \* \* \* \* \*

LOOKING ON THE BRIGHT SIDE OF LIFE
WILL NEVER CAUSE EYESTRAIN.

\* \* \* \* \* \*

Most of us miss out on life's big prizes.
   The Pulitzer.
   The Heisman.
   Oscars.
But we're all eligible for life's small pleasures.
   A pat on the back.
   A kiss behind the ear.
   A four-pound bass.
   A full moon.
   An empty parking space.
   A crackling fire.
   A great meal.
   A glorious sunset.
Enjoy life's tiny delights.
There are plenty for all of us.

                 Source unknown

\* \* \* \* \* \*

FAITH IS PUTTING ALL YOUR EGGS IN GOD'S BASKET
AND COUNTING YOUR BLESSINGS
BEFORE THEY'VE HATCHED.

\*    \*    \*    \*    \*    \*

A SMILE IS A WRINKLE
THAT SHOULDN'T BE REMOVED.

\*    \*    \*    \*    \*    \*

A SMILE IS THE LIGHTING SYSTEM OF THE FACE
AND THE HEATING SYSTEM OF THE HEART.

\*    \*    \*    \*    \*    \*

A SMILE IS A LIGHT IN THE WINDOW OF YOUR FACE
THAT SHOWS THAT YOUR HEART IS AT HOME.

\*    \*    \*    \*    \*    \*

When you talk, do not say harmful things. But say what people need—words that will help others become stronger. (Eph. 4:29, NCV)

# How to Lay Down Your Agonies and Pick Up Your Credentials

*You have to face the music before you can lead the band.*

Smiling between disasters is a good start in finding splashes of joy, but surviving in the cesspool—and eventually climbing out—takes the ability to deal with pain and grief. Nothing comes into our lives by accident; and no matter how bad it makes you feel, it didn't come to stay—it came to pass!

The hard part is dealing with being alive while waiting for whatever it is to pass. When pain and grief capsize your life, it sometimes seems that all you can do is sink. Sometimes the pain comes through the finality of death. The following are just a few excerpts of the many letters I receive from people whose lives have been shattered by loss:

One month and one week ago today our oldest child, Jeff, age eleven, collapsed in sudden death due to myocarditis (a nonsymptomatic disease of the heart muscle caused by a virus). We are having tremendous support from our church here and from neighbors and co-workers, but my world is shattered. My heart is torn in half. One half is grateful that he knew the

23

Lord . . . he is safe and happy in heaven with Jesus. But the human half of my heart longs for Jeff. . . . I walked the four miles to the cemetery and back this morning. I sat by Jeff's grave and cried and prayed and remembered.

\*   \*   \*   \*   \*   \*

Last summer while purchasing a book, I saw *So Stick a Geranium in Your Hat and Be Happy*. I was still in shock after my daughter's murder, a period of my life that is still a total blur. I thought, "Why not?" and bought it. That night I read it and laughed for one of the few times since Melanie's kidnapping and torture-killing by a couple of idiots who thought themselves to be high priests in a cult.

Your pain was not the exact replica of our pain, but pain for mothers is universal when it comes to the death of a child.

Another mother wrote to tell of having one daughter who developed cystic fibrosis and became so ill she was confined to a wheelchair. While this mother and her husband did all they could to make life happy for their daughter, she died at age fifteen. They tried for another child, and a year later a second daughter was born. Then, two years later, a surprise package came—a third little girl. Then the roller coaster took another plunge. "We were doing okay in life until March," the mother wrote. "Then SIDS [Sudden Infant Death Syndrome] hit our family and we lost our new daughter in her sleep. Life seems too hard."

When letters like these arrive—and they keep coming all the time—it helps me understand why I went through my own cesspools of pain. Those terrible times helped me earn the credentials that now enable me to help others deal with their pain as I continue to deal with my own troubles and the bittersweet memories that are like embedded shrapnel deep in my heart.

You see, memories are always there, a permanent part of our lives, and unless we can deal with them, they will continue to cause pain and grief that will cripple us. That's why it's important to make all the good memories we can *while* we can. Then when the bitter things happen, there will be enough sweet memories to absorb the shock and put a coating of love around the shrapnel, blunting its sharp edges.

When I look at my own tragedies, I realize they all involve the men in my life—the men I love the most. I have told thousands of people, in person and in print, about four of these tragedies: the devastating accident that almost left my husband blind and comatose, like a vegetable; the violent deaths of two of my four sons; and finally, the discovery that another son is gay.

All of this happened in a period of nine years, ripping apart the happy family that Bill and I had established together. I believe, however, that I started learning about how to deal with pain and bittersweet memories earlier in life. When I was twelve, my father was taken from us one night, quickly and silently, the way a heart attack often strikes.

### "I'll Bring You Some Black Jack Gum"

My dad was the Associate Pastor of the Calvary Undenominational Church in Grand Rapids, Michigan, serving with the Senior Pastor, Dr. M. R. DeHaan. I'll never forget the night Daddy left for a board meeting at the church. It was still early in the evening and my mother, sister, and I were listening to the old Horace Heidt radio program, "A Pot of Gold," featuring calls to homes across America picked in random fashion from the phone book. As we sat there listening, we were waiting for the phone to ring, thinking it might be our call for the $1,000 Pot of Gold.

A call did come before the program was over, but the caller wasn't Horace Heidt. It was my dad, who told my mother he wasn't feeling too well, but he had taken some Tums and was still planning to attend the meeting. Then he got me on the phone and asked, "What can I bring you when I come home tonight?"

"I'd like some Black Jack gum," I said instantly.

My father laughed because he knew how much I loved Black Jack gum. I not only loved the licorice taste, but I had fun getting it smeared over my teeth and making it look as if some of my teeth were missing.

Once, while riding in the car with my parents, they came up behind a truck and wanted to pass, but the trucker wouldn't let us. He seemed to enjoy teasing me as I looked out the window at him. As usual, I was chewing a big wad of Black Jack gum and I decided to coat my teeth with it and give him a big "smile." I guess it startled him so much he decided to let my father go on by; as we went on down the road I could see him laughing at my black, "toothless" grin.

My father hung up, chuckling after promising he would bring me some Black Jack gum. Then he went back to his meeting and we went back to listening to "Pot of Gold."

When the program ended (and once again we hadn't received the lucky call) my sister and I went off to bed and later my mother did, as well. About midnight there was a knock at our door. It was Dr. DeHaan and a deacon from church. "I'm sorry," he said. "Your husband had one crushing chest pain and then it was over! There was nothing we could do for him."

I can still remember Dr. DeHaan's voice from down in the hallway telling my mother that Daddy was dead. The rest of the night is a blur in my memory now, except for two other sounds: my mother making the phone calls to relatives, and the mourning doves chirping in the trees about 3:00 or 4:00 A.M. They made such an ominous, lonely sound . . .

## The Memories Kept Flooding Back

Sleep wouldn't come that night. I thought of my dad and how much he loved me. One thing that came to my mind was that whenever I got an earache, my dad would go out and buy a cigar, even though he never smoked. One of the old-fashioned remedies for earache was to blow cigar smoke into the ear to relieve the pain. My dad would practically make himself sick smoking that cigar and blowing smoke in my ear. And even now, when I see a man with a cigar, I remember Dad puffing on one while he held me and gently blew smoke in my ear.

I have all kinds of memories of my dad. Some of our best fun happened in the car. Often I'd ride with him and he'd drill me on Bible verses. He taught a Scripture memorization class on Saturday mornings at church, and he decided it would be good for me to learn all the verses perfectly as well, including the "addresses." And so wherever I went with him in the car he'd rehearse me on quoting the verse and then giving the reference.

Whenever we drove out to see my grandmother, who lived some twenty miles away in the country, we'd take a road that had big dips. And I mean really BIG DIPS. My dad knew how I loved to go over those dips in the car. While my mother didn't care for the game at all, he'd tell me to sit down on the floor by the backseat, which accentuated the feeling of going over the dips. We'd zoom over the road and I'd laugh and he'd laugh with me. Coming back from Grandma's we'd do it again, until we were both laughing so hard we were almost hysterical.

Recently, when I was back in Michigan, I had occasion to go over that same road, but today it's a nice smooth freeway with no dips at all. In my mind, however, the dips will always be there, and I'll always remember how my dad would take all the time in the world to go over those dips, back and forth, just so we could laugh and make memories that would last a lifetime.

Those memories flashed through my mind that night my dad died, and I lay in the darkness, crying and wondering what would happen to us. The next morning, after they had taken my father's body to the mortuary, someone came by to drop off the clothes he had been wearing when he died. In his pocket were several packs of Black Jack gum he had bought—just for me.

## They Put Daddy in the Sun Room

When my dad died in 1940, it was the custom to bring the body back to the home after it had been prepared by the mortuary and placed in the casket. Then friends would come to visit, bring food, sit around and talk, and show their care and concern before the actual funeral.

We had what we called a "sun room" at our house, and I remember that it was there we put Daddy. I remember hearing Mother say, "Daddy always liked that room," and I thought, *as if it matters now.*

Up until that time I had never seen a dead person—I was only twelve. I didn't want to touch him or kiss him. All I could do was look at his cold, still body. It was my first encounter with the stark reality of death.

My mother said I had to get a new dress for the funeral, and I still remember the navy blue, print dress she picked out for me. Because I had sung with my dad a lot in church, Mom asked me to pick out the songs to be sung at his funeral. I chose "Under His Wings" and "Constantly Abiding," staid old hymns he had liked. I don't hear those hymns much today, but occasionally I'll be in a church that uses older hymnals and they will be sung. Then my mind will flash back fifty years as the words of those old songs bring back the memories.

Even as I write about my father's death, the memories are still there, pieces of shrapnel embedded in my heart. They are not "haunting memories"; instead, they're bittersweet because the pain has been dulled and flattened out with time. What makes it possible to bear the painful part of the memories are the sweet memories that have surrounded the shrapnel with love. That's why I call them "bittersweet."


**No More Tragedy Until . . .**

While my father's death was a tremendous blow to our family and my mother had to struggle over the next several years, I grew up and went through high school and college with no more tragedy. I got out of college and married Bill after meeting him on a blind date. If it's true that opposites attract, then Bill and I were destined to get married because we were, and still are, TOTAL opposites.

Bill had an excellent job in mechanical engineering, and God also blessed us with four sons, a comfortable home, a growing church, a swimming pool, two cats, and a dog. The years were sprinkled with normal stresses until 1966, when things started happening that turned our lives into a nightmare.*

On the night we left for our church retreat where we were to be counselors for the young people, Bill had gone on ahead of me, taking the food and other supplies. About twenty minutes later, I followed in our other car with all the children.

As I drove up the dark, curving, mountain road, I came upon a heap of a man lying on the roadway, covered with blood and glass. The only way I could tell it was Bill was by his clothing. The road had not been used all winter, and evidently he had hit some debris left behind by a construction crew.

Quickly, I jumped out of the car and, after making sure Bill was alive, I knew I had to get help fast. I left one of the older boys with him there on the road and drove ten miles to get to a telephone to call an ambulance. When it came, I rode with Bill to the hospital, leaving the children with friends from the church. Then I waited all night to get some word about his prognosis.

About 6:00 A.M. I went home alone and walked into an empty house. There was no Bill, no kids. I had no idea what I would do if he didn't make it. What if he did live but his brain was so damaged it couldn't work? Our lives had been clicking along very smoothly and now, suddenly, our family had gone from click to CLUNK. Nothing fit. Nothing worked. Nothing clicked any more.

Two days later the neurosurgeon and ophthalmologist gave me their verdict. Bill was blind and was having continual seizures from severe brain damage. They said his condition was "unrehabilitatable," a word I was to hear many times over the next few months. Because Bill was a veteran, the doctors advised me to have him admitted to Sawtelle Veterans Hospital because he would never fit into a family unit again. Bill, they

---

*The tragedies discussed in this chapter are described in further detail in two other books, *Where Does A Mother Go to Resign?* (Minneapolis: Bethany House Publishers, 1979), and *So, Stick a Geranium in Your Hat and Be Happy* (Dallas: Word Publishing, 1990).

said, would be a vegetable because of his irreversible brain damage, and he had five years to live, at most.

It turned out that it would be several months before a bed opened up at Sawtelle; so, after several weeks in intensive care, we brought Bill home to try and manage there. He was blind and he didn't know us; his memory was gone. I was able to locate someone to stay with Bill while I went out to apply for Social Security, his veteran's pension, disability, and Aid to the Blind. I even got Bill a white cane and a whole stack of records to listen to.

It was a slow process. Many people were praying, but there were plenty of nights when I wondered what would happen to all of us. How could I raise four sons and take care of Bill, too? He had always been in control—had always been such a perfectionistic person about handling the details of life. Now my strong, strapping husband had been reduced to a helpless invalid.

Then, after I managed to get Bill on all the various programs and enough money coming in to pay expenses, God healed him! He regained his sight, and his mind started to function. He finally recognized who we were, and some psychological therapy restored a great deal of his memory.

## Where There's Smoke, There Should Be Smell

Even though Bill was slowly getting better, it was necessary to have someone there all the time for absolute safety. I learned this one day when I popped out to the supermarket for a few minutes to grab some groceries, thinking it would be safe enough to leave Bill alone that long.

What I didn't realize was that the accident had destroyed Bill's sense of smell. When I drove back up to the house, the roof was in flames! Dashing in, I found Bill there in the back bedroom, lying peacefully in his back brace, seemingly content with life.

"I've got to call the fire department," I shouted. "The house is on fire!"

"What?" Bill said. "I don't smell any smoke . . ."

The fire department came in just a few minutes and managed to extinguish the roof before the house went up in flames. They determined that somehow a bird had picked up a lighted cigarette somewhere and deposited it under one of our wood shingles. By the time I had gotten back from the market, the roof was ablaze.

As I looked at Bill lying there in his back brace, without sight or smell, I thought back to when he had been whole and our lives had been whole, as well. Because he had been a pilot during World War II, he enjoyed watching old war movies. He loved to see the planes and hear the roar of the engines.

Popcorn was Bill's favorite. One day while we were at Knott's Berry Farm he stopped in one of the shops and bought a giant earthenware bowl that looked big enough to be a bathtub for one of the kids. Bill loved to make popcorn on Friday nights and fill that bowl to the brim; then we'd all sit there eating it together, watching television.

Sweet memories like those helped me get through the first bitter years following Bill's injuries. I honestly can't remember doing a lot of grieving during those months following Bill's accident. I experienced a lot of anguish, frustration, and pressure, but I was really too busy to grieve. I kept praying that, somehow, Bill would recover, even though specialists had said he was unrehabilitatable.

You can imagine our sheer joy as we watched God do miracles before our eyes. Bill's vision returned, and he was even able to go back to work as an engineer. Our family's ship had been practically capsized by a hurricane, but God had righted things and we were getting back in balance. Of course, Bill was still a bit strange, but I didn't mind. He is an only child and they are all a little bit different anyway!

## The Pain Had Just Begun

Actually, the pain I had experienced up until then was only a taste of what lay ahead. In the next five years I would lose two of my sons, one to enemy fire in Vietnam and another to a drunk driver whose three-ton truck would swerve across the center line on the Alaska Highway in the Yukon Territory. Each boy's death was different, yet each was the same.

During his senior year of high school, seventeen-year-old Steve became bored and restless. He was a Christian, but he started running with friends that we knew were into drugs and drinking. In the fall of 1967, he continued to pressure Bill and me to sign papers allowing him to join the marines because several of his friends had already gone in.

Neither Bill nor I was sold on the idea, but we were encouraged by news reports that seemed to be saying the Vietnam conflict was decelerating. Realizing that he could join on his own on his eighteenth birthday in December, I went down in October and signed the papers that made it possible for Steve to become a U.S. Marine.

Steve went off to boot camp, filled with fantasies of excitement and adventure, but within a few weeks he changed his mind. His letters began telling us the marines weren't as great as he had thought and he had doubts about being a marine after all.

A few weeks after Christmas that year, the Vietnam War burst into new levels of conflict. One bittersweet memory, forever a "freeze frame" in my mind, is Steven, with duffel bag over his shoulder, turning to wave to me before disappearing beyond the chain-link gates of Camp Pendleton as he left for Vietnam.

It was St. Patrick's Day, March 17, 1968, and it was the last time I was to see him alive. Five months later I would have to go identify his swollen, bloated body, which had turned a sickly brown from lying face down for two days in a rice paddy before being found. Leaving the mortuary, I knew this was no dream; this was REALITY. My grief was overwhelming, but over the following weeks and months I was able to accept what had happened by recalling bittersweet memories of Steve and how much fun we had enjoyed together. Those memories helped me get through the first stage of my loss.

### The Hearse Came Complete with Shovel and Spade

Steve and I used to find many things we could laugh about. Maybe it was because we both had the same warped sense of humor. One time he and I were driving home from church, and we went by a car lot where a big, black Cadillac hearse was for sale for $350.

"Wow!" Steve exclaimed. "Look at that hearse—wouldn't it be great to have something like that?"

Steve hadn't had his driver's license too long, and I'm sure he never dreamed that I would consider buying the hearse. We stopped and talked to the salesman and learned that the car had been brought to California from Minnesota. The interior was a beautiful purple velvet. There was even a compartment near the back, and inside it was a shovel *and* a spade!

It was obvious Steve really wanted that hearse. Bill had already driven home from church with our other boys, and I decided to make a snap decision. I wrote out a check for $350 and bought the hearse. Steve could hardly contain himself as he drove it home.

When we got there, Bill could hardly contain himself, either—but not out of great glee. It took some fast talking to get him to let Steve keep the hearse. We really couldn't afford it at the time because Bill was still in recovery from his accident; but "anything for fun"—and the hearse was a lot of fun, indeed.

Steve's friends were enthralled with the hearse. They wanted to sit in it, drive it, and try out the shovel and spade. It only got six miles to the gallon, but being a good businessman, Steve managed to make a few dollars by renting it to some of his buddies for Halloween. They decorated it and had a great time driving it up and down, "haunting" the boulevard. I still have photos of Halloween night, as well as pictures of Steve and his friends heading for the beach in his hearse, with surfboards hanging out the back!

Bittersweet memories like that helped me get through our loss of Steve, as did sharing with other families who had lost sons in Vietnam. Using a list of names printed in the daily paper, we contacted families who had lost their sons in the war and started sharing our hope and faith with them.

Eventually, I began to tell myself that surely we had had our cup of suffering. Bill had recovered from what doctors called hopeless injuries. While his memory wasn't too good (he would still watch old John Wayne movies over and over, not realizing he had seen them before), he was functioning at work and was pretty well back to normal. Steve had been killed in Vietnam and was our deposit in heaven. Now we could go on with our lives. But as one saying puts it,

> LIFE IS WHAT HAPPENS
> AFTER YOU MAKE OTHER PLANS.

What would happen next was so unbelievable it was unthinkable. Violent death would take our Tim at a time when he was experiencing an excitement about spiritual things that he had never known before and when all of a productive life seemed ahead of him.

### Tim's Sense of Humor Was "Different"

Ironically, many memories of Tim also include a hearse— not the one we bought for Steve, but a pink one he drove for his employer, a mortuary. Our first-born son was a serious, conscientious kid who wasn't into fun quite as much as the rest of us. His idea of something hilarious was to bring home bows from the funeral bouquets and decorate one of our dogs or our cat with "REST IN PEACE," or "GOD BLESS GRANDPA HIRAM."

When I spoke in the Northwest recently and told about Tim bringing home the BOWS from the mortuary to decorate the dog and cat, a darling little old lady came up afterward and said, "Mrs. Johnson, I feel so bad to think your son brought home the BONES from the mortuary." I tried to reassure her that Tim had never brought home any bones—only BOWS.

Tim would sometimes stop at home while on duty and have lunch, leaving the hearse (with one of its latest occupants) parked in the driveway. One day he took his little brother, Barney, to the mortuary. Making sure no one was around, Tim let Barney climb into an empty casket in one of the viewing rooms—just to see what it felt like. Then (just for fun) he shut the lid!

Barney let out a yelp and Tim opened the lid in a few seconds—after he had a good laugh, of course.

The next day Barney went to school and during sharing time he told his class what had happened. Barney's teacher listened to his incredible tale and later phoned me to say, "Mrs. Johnson, I don't like to tell you this, but I'm afraid Barney is starting to tell lies. He's coming up with stories that just *can't* be true!"

When she told me what Barney had said, I reassured her that Barney wasn't lying and that my college-age son just had a "different" sense of humor. But I'm not sure I totally convinced her.

Although he lacked what I call a "fun personality," Tim had no trouble attracting the young ladies. Tall and handsome, he always had several girlfriends; they would often come over for a swim in our pool. Another "freeze frame" tucked away in my memory is a giant inner tube floating in our pool with no one in sight. Tim and his girlfriend would be inside the inner tube, but it was so huge I couldn't see them. So, every now and then, I would go out to the pool just to check on them.

### Tim's Last Call—a Bittersweet Memory

My most bittersweet memory of Tim was the last conversation I had with him—on the day he was killed. He was calling from Whitehorse, Yukon Territory (collect, of course), to tell me he and his friend, Ron, were heading home after spending the summer working and making friends in a church they particularly liked. What struck me most was Tim's voice. Instead of the calm, unexcited tone he usually had, he was bubbling with enthusiasm because of what God had been doing in his life.

"Mom, I've got a sparkle in my eye and a spring in my step," he said. "I don't have time to tell you about it now, but God's going to use my story all over! I'll see you in five days!"

But it wasn't to be. A few hours later, as we sat at dinner talking about Tim's call, the phone rang and a Royal Canadian Mounted Police officer told me my son and his friend were dead. Their little Volkswagen had been crushed by a three-ton truck with a drunken driver at the wheel.

The wounds of grief that had only partially healed from Steve's death five years before were now ripped open again and deeper than ever. I thought I had accepted Steve's death. He was our one deposit in heaven. Why did God need TWO?

Ten days later, I made my second trip up to the mortuary to identify another dead boy in a box. This trip was as unreal as the first. The mortician had called and said, "Mrs. Johnson, this is the first time I have ever had to call THE SAME FAMILY twice, but you'll have to come up here and identify Tim's body because he was killed in a foreign country."

Because Bill still wasn't getting around much, I drove alone to the mortuary. Incredibly, it had been just five years to that VERY DAY that I'd gone to identify Steve's body—also killed in a foreign country. It had been a hot day in August five years before when I had driven up this same road. Now, on another hot August day, I was even driving the same car (we don't change cars that often) to go look at ANOTHER boy in a box. I simply could not accept it. How could this be happening AGAIN? It was like a dream—no, a nightmare!

The memorial service for Tim and his friend glorified God in many ways as several of Tim's friends and classmates came to Christ. Christian magazines, including *Christian Life*, picked up the story and ran headlines like "Their Death Was Only a Beginning."

I was thankful for all the good that came out of our tragedy, but it really didn't dilute the pain. I thought I had learned something about dealing with grief with Steven's death, but Tim's death showed me that grief is a stern schoolmaster, and you always have to learn how to deal with it on your own. There is no course you can take, no book you can read, no video you can watch. You are your own video, moving slowly across the screen, feeling your way through your part in a tragic drama. At times like that, you wish your life were like a VCR and you could FAST FORWARD through the parts you don't want to live through.

## We All Grieve Differently

As I worked through the death of two sons, I developed some guidelines for dealing with grief. I learned these guidelines by trial and error—mostly error because my eyes were blinded with tears.

While there are certain stages of grief that everyone goes through, no two of us pass through these stages at the same pace or in the same way. When a loved one dies, the first stage of grief includes SHOCK, particularly if the death was not anticipated.

In Steve's case, he was in the midst of a war and we were aware that he could be taken at any moment because he was in a red-hot danger zone. When the news about Steve came, it was not nearly the shock that we experienced when we got that phone call telling us Tim had been killed in a car crash on the very day we were so excitedly anticipating his homecoming.

When the call came about Tim, I remember screaming through the house, "This CANNOT be . . . I just talked to him a couple of hours ago . . . He was on his way HOME!"

I could not believe that Tim was actually gone, crushed to death by a drunken driver. It simply could not BE. It had to be a nightmare or my imagination.

Shock is God's way of cushioning those He loves against tragedy. Going into shock gives you time to absorb what has happened so you can try to adjust to the news.

## When Shock Wears Off, Pain Begins

Grief is to the emotions what surgery is to the body. Once the anesthetic of shock wears off, the PAIN can be intense. How long that pain lasts is different in each person's case. There is no time limit. Also, the grieving person must understand:

GRIEF CANNOT BE DRY CLEANED AWAY;
IT MUST BE WASHED IN TEARS.

In Spatula Ministries we deal for the most part with grief-stricken mothers, but we also deal with a certain number of dads. I'm glad to see that our society is becoming more permissive about thinking it's okay for a man to cry. I have a friend who told me about her son—a mature, married man who was the father of three children of his own. The day he heard on the radio that President John F. Kennedy had been shot to death, this grown man fled to his mother's house, burst through the door, buried his head on her shoulder, and sobbed like a child.

For this man, coming home to his mother and weeping symbolized comfort, warmth, and security—all the things little children get from their mommies. This big, strong six-footer wanted to cry openly and relieve himself from the inner pain and shock. And where else could he go but HOME, where there was security, where tears were understood without any questions?

If you're grieving, perhaps you will get the most help from those who are comfortable with their own tears, as well as yours. Tears are the lowest common denominator of humanity. As Helmuth Pleaser has said, "More forcefully than any other expression or emotion, the crying of our fellow man grips and makes us partners of his moment, often without even knowing why."

God reads the heart, and He understands the language of tears. You can find many wonderful verses about tears and weeping in the Psalms. For example, David wrote, "Record my lament; list my tears on your scroll—are they not in your record?" (Ps. 56:8, NIV).

A possible translation for this verse says that the psalmist asks God to put his tears in God's bottle, or wineskin. It is as if he knows that his tears will be precious to God, that God will preserve them, honor them, and eventually heal them.

## It's Okay to Grieve

Some Christians make the mistake of thinking that grief isn't a "good testimony." They are on the ceiling, climbing the wall, or prostrate before the Lord in their grief, but they feel guilty about it. I agree with the writer who said: "Grief is not a sign of weakness, but a tribute to the loved one and a healthy response to our heartache. Avoiding grief postpones recovery. Clinging to grief prolongs pain. Neither approach helps us heal."[1]

That's good advice, but unfortunately, some well-meaning Christian friends can subtly imply that "grieving is *not* okay." When Tim died, people dropped by and tried to say all the right things, such as, "How wonderful it is that Tim is now with the Lord." Someone else mentioned that it was "good that you still have two children left." While I appreciated the intentions of these remarks, they didn't comfort me at all—they only worsened my wounds that were already more raw and bleeding.

Yes, I knew it was wonderful that Tim was with the Lord, but I wanted Tim home with us—with me, his mother, who had borne him, raised him, and loved him. As for having two sons left, yes, that was good also; but I wanted Tim, too! Now he was our second deposit in heaven, and I was wondering how much God would demand of us. Was Larry or Barney NEXT? But I really couldn't tell my friends these things because they wouldn't understand.

## Grief Will Make You Angry

Recently, a mother wrote to me about her only son, Jeff, who was killed in an accident over four years ago. She had heard I was writing another book and she said:

> If, in your new book, you could help those in grief over los-ing a child. We still need help. It's like one day you cope and the next day you can't. If you could please tell us how you and Bill have coped after losing two sons. Do you ever get angry at God? Do you want to punch out people? Do people bug you? It's hard to see other families with their loved ones. I get re-sentful. I want to believe and yet doubts come in. To love God is sometimes hard. People say busy hands will help, but, Barb, sometimes you have to put your hands down—and then you cry. I have a good husband and two lovely daughters. I want to help them, but I seem lost.

In addition to shock and pain, another natural reaction to the death of a loved one is ANGER, particularly if death strikes from out of the blue, without any warning, and for what seems to be no reason. When my shock turned into pain over Tim's death, anger immediately welled up within me. Because my "Ivory-soap" Christian friends didn't seem to understand me, I would get in the car late at night and drive to a dump a few miles from our house. There I could grieve in private, without having to dodge their "Bible bullets."

Today that dump has gates, and no parking is allowed there at night because the police fear that someone could be mugged, or worse. But in 1973, the dump was open, and I would park there and just sob my heart out. Sometimes I would scream to let God know how I felt. I told God how angry I was with folks who kept telling me that I should be glad Tim is with Him. And I also told God how angry I was because Tim had been taken. "WHY, Lord?" I would ask. "Tim was so precious, so special, and he had just renewed his faith in YOU! What glory could it bring to have him DIE?"

When I share my story of going to the dump to grieve, and even to rant and rave at God, many parents tell me that they feel somewhat relieved because I have admitted that I was so MAD at God for losing my sons. I tell them that it is okay to express these emotions and it is okay to be mad at God. When we scream in agony and rage at Him through our grief, He doesn't say, "Off to hell with you, Sister!" Instead, He patiently loves us . . . carries us . . . wraps His blanket of tenderness around us while we are balking, hissing, and rebelling in every way.

You see, God gave us our ability to have emotions. They are part of our lives, and they are normal. Anger, wrath, wanting to kill someone (even yourself), and flailing away at God for letting this happen to you—these are all normal emotional feelings that aren't necessarily a final commentary on your spiritual condition. The Bible says that we should be slow to become angry and that anger does not bring about the righteous life that God desires (see James 1:19, 20); but it seems to me that this passage is talking about the kind of anger that comes out of pride, bitterness, and carrying a grudge.

Anger that comes out of pain and grief is a normal response to deep hurt. This kind of hurt is the same whether or not you are a Christian. If your leg is amputated, it hurts—no matter what your spiritual values may be. It is vital to understand that having emotional pain is okay, but *you must not leave it there inside yourself.* You must find ways to ventilate your feelings, and then healing can begin because:

OPENNESS IS TO WHOLENESS
AS SECRETS ARE TO SICKNESS.

You are only as sick as your secrets. All of us experience a kaleidoscope of emotions and they are all useful when they are directed in healthy ways. That includes anger. We can learn to drain our anger by releasing it. Then we feel better and can start to pick up the broken fragments of our lives. It's better to vent your anger at God than at other family members or your friends. God can take it, but your human loved ones may not be able to accept what you are saying.

So, if you are angry, let it out. Go into your room, pound on your pillow, and DRAIN SOME OF THOSE EMOTIONS. You may even want to sob without trying to stifle the sounds (more on this in chapter 3). You will find that as you ventilate your anger, you will dilute it, and eventually it won't be there any more. By ventilating it, you get your feelings out; then you can begin a cleansing of your heart and the slow process of mending. As you replace angry feelings with tenderness and forgiveness, you will experience healing.

The most important thing is to DRAIN YOUR PAIN, release your anger much as a safety valve releases steam. I love the "tantrum mat" that appears on page 43. I've included it in my *Love Line* newsletter, along with the directions for how to throw a tantrum. Obviously, it's just for fun, but it still carries a very deep truth. You need to let out your pain. As for "persisting symptoms" and seeing a Christian counselor, that's a possibility. I had those symptoms, myself, and in the next chapter I'll share that experience with you.

## Grief Comes to Pass; It Doesn't Stay

You will get better and pass into the RECOVERY stage. Widowed twice herself, Ida Fisher, co-author of *The Widow's Guide to Life*, says three T's are essential to recovering from the loss of a loved one:

TEARS, TALK, AND TIME[2]

As true inner-healing takes place, all that is left is an emotional scar as a reminder of what happened. The dawn of hope will break over the darkness of grief. You can talk about the loved one who's gone and begin to cherish the memories instead of having the memories tear out your insides. Instead of feeling like embedded shrapnel, the bittersweet memories will be marinated in love. And soon you will be able to reach out to others who are in pain.

# TANTRUM
# MAT

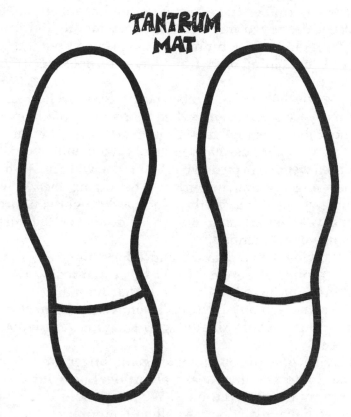

Directions: —
When the need for throwing a tantrum
is felt, place both feet on the space
provided and jump rapidly up and
down. Incoherent screaming is
also permissible. If symptoms
persist, see your nearest
psychiatrist — you MAY be a nut.

After Steve's death, we started helping other parents who had lost sons in Vietnam. When Tim died, the ministry expanded beyond the parents of casualties from Vietnam; soon I was sharing with parents who had lost children in auto accidents or other tragedies. Grief had changed me, but it had not destroyed me. God had held me up and brought me through the dark tunnel. As the psalmist put it, He was indeed "my hiding place from every storm of life" (Ps. 32:7, TLB).

When dealing with parents who are grieving, I explain that the recovery stage begins when you wake up one morning without that overwhelming urge to go back to bed and pull up the covers. It does happen; the heavy mantle of grief that has been weighing you down is lifted. You will actually be able to hear music again. The birds will be singing, the sun will be shining, you will realize that God has brought you through. You have survived, and you can lay down your agonies and pick up your credentials.

Following Tim's death, I had opportunities to speak to many groups of parents. I told them that losing two sons had brought incredible pain but that the pain was easing and I could actually feel God's comforting blanket of love around me. I could finally accept having *two* deposits in heaven.

Having gone through shock, pain, anger, and recovery twice, I had begun to learn about dealing with the grief caused by losing loved ones. We are to hold loosely to all that we have, realizing it is all so temporary. Our possessions—even our children—are all loaned to us. God can pluck the flowers for His garden whenever He chooses. We are only the caretakers. Sometimes it gives a better perspective if we can accept that everything we have is only on loan anyway.

But I still had more to learn. Life has a way of dealing new, even harder, blows. That's the way it was for me. One very important lesson still lay ahead.

## Splish/Splash . . .

> You are His gem—
> Tested, shining and sparkling.
> You have survived the winds of adversity . . .
> You are a WINNER!
> You are an OVERCOMER!
> YOU HAVE CREDENTIALS!
>
> Source unknown

\*    \*    \*    \*    \*    \*

TO ALL PARENTS

"I'll lend you for a little time a child of Mine," He said,
"For you to love the while she lives and mourn for when
    she's dead.
It may be six or seven years, or twenty-two or three,
But will you, till I call her back, take care of her for Me?
She'll bring her charms to gladden you, and shall her
    stay be brief
You'll have her lovely memories as solace for your grief.

"I cannot promise she will stay, since all from earth
    return,
But there are lessons taught down there I want this child
    to learn.
I've looked the wide world over in my search for
    teachers true
And from the throngs that crowd life's lanes I have
    selected you.
Now will you give her all your love, nor think the labor
    vain,
Nor hate Me when I come to call to take her back
    again?"

I fancied that I heard them say: "Dear Lord, Thy will be
    done!

For all the joy Thy child shall bring, the risk of grief we'll
    run.
We'll shelter her with tenderness, we'll love her while
    we may,
And for the happiness we've known forever grateful
    stay;
But shall the angels call for her much sooner than we've
    planned,
We'll brave the bitter grief that comes and try to under-
    stand."

Edgar A. Guest[3]

\*    \*    \*    \*    \*    \*

Trouble is not a sign of inadequacy, stupidity or inferiority,
but rather an inescapable part of life—proof that you are a card-
carrying member of the human race.

Ann Landers[4]

\*    \*    \*    \*    \*    \*

I will . . . transform her Valley of Troubles into a Door of
Hope. (Hos. 2:15, TLB)

# We Must Understand That It Is Not Always Necessary to Understand

*Can this really be my life,*
*or has there been some mistake?*
Ashleigh Brilliant[1]

As hard as it was to lose two sons, eventually there was a closure in their deaths and that closure became my ally. But it took time to reach that point. For weeks, the "Why me's?" still rang in my mind—especially after Tim was killed. "Why me?" is a natural part of grief. Read this letter one man wrote to God after he learned his son was born blind:

God, You seem very far from me right now. I really don't feel like praying to You at all. But then, again, maybe I'm afraid of what I'm going to say. All my life I've carefully chosen my words when I prayed. I wanted to impress You with my sincerity and goodness. But today I'm very angry, the angriest I've ever been with You. You know how much I have wanted a baby. I prayed that the baby would be born healthy. Well, God, he is blind. HE'S BLIND! How can I ever again believe that You are a loving God? What infuriates me more is that my neighbor, an atheist, has four strapping kids. It isn't fair, God. I do blame You for this loss.

We need to give our anger to God. Job, after losing his family in a violent storm, hurled his anger at God, but God understood. The Bible tells us we should grieve, but not as those who grieve without hope. Yes, we DO blame God for some of our losses. We should not feel guilty telling Him we are angry, but as our anger cools we can learn a valuable lesson about a monstrous myth—that faith in God is an insurance policy with the feature clause being God's protection from severe blows. We forget we are living in a broken world with broken lives, broken hearts, broken dreams. What a spiritual flaw it is to think that becoming a Christian gives us immunity from this pain.

Some things we will never understand. Some losses will never make sense to us, but in time and in God's economy we can see that Romans 8:28 is true and does work. All things DO work together for good for those who love God.

We have biblical principles to live by and wise friends to give us counsel, yet we cannot always find an answer to all the pain. Some of us will die, never knowing the "Why?" of our lives. We will have to be content realizing, "The secret things belong to the LORD . . ." (Deut. 29:29, NIV).

### Does God Ever Have to Say, "Oops"?

We may never know the answer to the puzzling questions of life, but does it matter? Do we stop praying because our prayers were not answered as we wanted? In our case, we asked God to bring Tim safely home from his trip to Alaska, trusting that God would give him the "journey mercies" that we asked for. Within a few hours of our prayers, our son was smashed to death. Did this encourage our desire to pray? No. Did it make us think, *What is the use of it all anyway?* Of course it did. Why bother to pray when it did no good? He was killed even though we asked for his safety. Were we mad at God? Certainly. How unfair, how cruel, how crushing.

But lying deep beneath all of these feelings was our underlying faith that God makes no mistakes—that He never has to say, "Oops!" God didn't cause that drunken driver to cross the center line. Despite all of our questions and our bitter grief, however, we still knew, deep down, that nothing ever happens to us that God doesn't know about. God still loved us, and He was there for us in our grief, in our pain—and in our anger.

Tim was taken at a time when he was closer to God than he had been in his entire life. While we were grieving for Tim, a pastor visited us to tell us that the Scriptures say God plucks the flowers for His garden when they are most beautiful. At first I didn't want to hear it, but later that thought came to be a comfort to me.

And eventually the "Why me's?" stopped and the healing comfort of closure began. Yes, Tim was gone; yes, I missed him terribly. But slowly I worked through the grief of losing a second son and arrived at a kind of plateau where I could say, "Surely, two deposits in heaven is enough."

But there was still more to learn. In many ways, dealing with the deaths of two sons was my undergraduate course in grief. In the advanced course, I learned that there are not only different *stages* to grief; there are different *kinds* of grief. And I learned that even death does not necessarily bring the worst kind of pain.

## I Earned a Ph.D. in Pain

My postgraduate course in grief began the day I accidentally came upon homosexual pornography in Larry's dresser drawer.* Ironically, I made this discovery the morning after

---

* For more complete accounts of my struggles with discovering my son's homosexuality, see *So, Stick a Geranium in Your Hat and Be Happy* (Dallas: Word Publishing, 1990), chapters 3 and 11, and *Where Does a Mother Go to Resign?* (Minneapolis: Bethany House Publishers, 1979).

we had attended our twenty-year-old son's junior-college graduation exercises and watched him receive numerous awards, including Outstanding Student. One of the leading clergymen in California was the commencement speaker and he told us after the ceremonies, "God has His hand on this boy, and will use him in a special way."

When I found the homosexual material, as well as explicit letters written to Larry and sent to a post office box, I couldn't believe that all this garbage belonged to my son. Perhaps it was all for some kind of research project at school—the trouble was, school was over!

I was in shock as I drove to the airport to meet a plane carrying my sister and her husband, who were coming in for a special weekend celebration with our family. We were to be together for the first time since Tim's death.

I threw all of the pictures and letters into the trunk of my car and headed for the airport, sobbing and shaking in disbelief. My chest felt like an elephant was standing on it. I was churning inside, and the sounds coming out of my mouth were strange, choking sobs I had never heard before. It felt like a bull was goring me or a knife was being twisted violently back and forth in my heart.

All the way to the airport—almost an hour's drive—I groaned and wanted to throw up. I felt as if a shag rug had been shoved down my throat. At the same time, my teeth started to itch. My drive to the airport was awful, but it helped me let out some of the pain I was feeling inwardly, and that enabled me to get through the next few hours. Later that evening, I heard from Larry's own lips that he was, indeed, homosexual—or "maybe bisexual" (whatever that was. Homosexuality was in the Bible, but "bisexual"? I thought maybe it was someone who had sex twice a month. Why would he say THAT?)

My shock turned to anger and rage, and the next day Larry and I had a literal knock-down, drag-out confrontation in our living room. I screamed every Bible verse and word of condemnation I knew. He shouted back with every rebellious obscenity he could think of (many of which I had never heard before).

The following day Larry left in a fit of anger and did not come back or even contact us for almost a year. Then my rage soon turned to grief—my old, familiar tormenter—and the "Why me?" questions came back louder than ever. Folks asked me which was harder, losing two sons to death, or losing a boy into the gay lifestyle! As devastating as it was to bury two sons, it was even worse knowing another son was out there somewhere in a life so displeasing to God.

With Steve and Tim there had been grief, but there had also been closure. Good-byes were said, services were held, testimonies to God's glory were given, and graves were sealed. The raw edges of grief could heal because "it was over."

But in Larry's case, it was different. I was to be introduced to what so many parents have endured—long-term, continual grief.

Larry wasn't dead (although it might have been less hurtful that way). With the deaths of Steve and Tim had come support, friends dropping by, not always saying the right thing but at least saying SOMETHING to try to give comfort.

But who could I tell about Larry? Guilt turned me into a recluse. I dropped out of sight and stayed in my bedroom most of the time, counting the roses on my wallpaper and dwelling on bittersweet memories of how it used to be while Larry, who was in many ways the "apple of our eye," was growing up.

## Larry and I Always Loved to Laugh

Larry had been so musically talented, so caring, and always eager to have a laugh. When he was ten he was in a church Christmas program and was assigned to sing a solo, "While Shepherds Watched Their Flocks by Night." I helped Larry practice the song and sometimes he'd get silly and start using other words: "While shepherds washed their socks by night all seated on the ground, the angel of the Lord came down and said, 'Will you wash mine?'"

We were kidding around one day and Larry kept singing it the wrong way, just to get me laughing. Finally I said, "I'll give you five dollars if you get up in the program and sing it that way."

Larry laughed and said he wouldn't, of course, but on the night of the program he changed his mind—without telling us! He got out there in front of all the people and sure enough he started singing, "While shepherds washed their socks by night . . ."

He kept right on going with all the rest of the wrong words; but instead of being shocked the audience got tickled, and soon, everybody was laughing and clapping. Oh, yes, I did pay him the five dollars; the fun we had was worth it!

There were lots of other memories, too. We bought a player piano, and Larry loved to put on a honky-tonk tune and run his hands up and down the keyboard as if he were playing the song. I could recall talking to a repairman in our living room while Larry was at the piano. From where we stood, it looked to the repairman as though Larry were really playing up a storm. "Boy, that kid can really play!" said the repair man as he went on his way. As the door closed behind him, Larry and I dissolved in laughter.

As a teen-ager, Larry worked at In 'n' Out Burger, and he'd come home after the late-night shift with hamburgers for the two of us. We would sit together, watch Johnny Carson, eat hamburgers, and laugh. Larry had such a contagious, rippling laugh I'd have to tell him to be quiet or he'd wake up everyone.

And there was his little red Volkswagen with a wind-up key welded on the back. I'd chuckle every time I saw him drive off for school or work.

After Larry left and didn't contact us, I kept searching and hoping. Every time I saw a Volkswagen Bug, I'd look for the wind-up key, but I never spotted Larry's car.

## Living in the Shadows of Hope and Fear

As my anger about Larry turned into depression, the pain became intense. Pain usually has a physical cause, but it can also come out of deep mental or emotional hurts. In many ways, physical pain is easier to bear. But when you suffer emotional pain, you live in the alternating shadows of hope and fear. You hope you can get through this quickly and then you fear it will never end. While we always wish for a quick solution to our pain, we have to face the reality that there is no quick solution. When the hurt is deep and great, there is seldom an instant cure.

Pain goes on because the problem goes on. It might be betrayal by a spouse or a life-long friend; it might be injury from a serious accident that leaves you crippled or handicapped in some way. It could be some chronic problem in the family, like drug abuse, mental illness, or having a retarded child. And it can be, as it was in my case, a rebellious child who has broken your heart.

My mail comes predominantly from parents with long-lasting or chronic grief. One couple wrote to tell me about how they learned their thirty-year-old, talented, Christian, college-graduate, "never-gave-us-a-bit-of-trouble" son was a homosexual and had been exposed to the HIV virus. The mother's letter said, in part:

> I do not know how to describe how we felt then or even now because it is never the same for long. PAIN, anger, PAIN, guilt, PAIN, despair, PAIN, shame, PAIN, denial, PAIN, confusion, PAIN, loss, PAIN, fear, PAIN, numbness, and then it would begin all over again. My husband and I cried, prayed, talked, and hung on to each other. Each one trying to comfort the other when one was lower than the other. How could this be happening to us?

Just a few months later, this same mom and dad were numbed by another announcement. This time they learned that their twenty-seven-year-old, Christian, equally talented, college-graduate, "never-gave-us-a-bit-of-trouble" daughter

ALSO was a homosexual, but wasn't involved in a relationship at the time.

Since telling their parents that they are gay, both children
have moved several hundred miles away but remained in contact. They both say that they have never felt any differently,
that they have always been interested in only their same sex.
They also say that they want to find a partner and develop a
relationship that is as happy as their parents' marriage. The
mother's letter continues:

> So here we are at an impasse, too afraid and ashamed to tell
> [anyone] and dying inside because it is a very heavy burden.
> We know the Lord as our Savior and believe that all things work
> together for good to them that love Him and are called accord-
> ing to His purpose. So why are we having so much trouble turn-
> ing this whole mess over to Him? We agonize over what we
> must have done wrong to have both of our children turn out
> this way. I apologize for being so incoherent, but sometimes
> the pain is like a knife and I'm sure I will not survive—and I'm
> not so sure I even want to.

A letter like this shows that the term *heartbroken* is more
than just a metaphor. In the nineteenth century, some physi-
cians believed that severe grief could somehow damage the
heart and even bring on death. One doctor wrote, "Dissec-
tion of persons who have died shows congestion in and
inflammation of the heart with rupture of its auricles and
ventricles."[2]

Today, many doctors would agree that grief can literally
break your heart. And the letters I get verify it. The goal of
Spatula Ministries is found in Isaiah 61:1: "to bind up the brokenhearted . . ."(KJV).

Obviously, my broken heart didn't kill me, but it gave me
the same feeling that so many other mothers have described—
pain in the chest, as though a knife were being twisted around.

One mother told me that she had learned to live with that
knife in her chest by avoiding weddings, showers, or any other
festivities that reminded her of the son who had discarded his

family. That way, the knife didn't turn and twist as much. It was still there, but it was not destroying her.

When you are in pain like this, depression is ever present, or at least never far away. You need strength to just get through each day. "Why me?" becomes your favorite question. You know it's the wrong question to ask, but you can't help it.

Whoever coined the phrase "misery loves company" was right—to a point. Anyone in long-term pain and grief—caused by a wayward child, for example—is often drawn to others, especially other parents who have the same problem. That's why Spatula Ministries' support groups keep getting new members constantly. Parents sharing the same pain can identify with each other, opening up the abscesses, draining the pain by talking with others who understand because they are having the same feelings. It may not ease our pain to know that someone else hurts worse, but it does help to know that God measures our strength and allows us a heavy burden to stretch and strengthen us a day at a time.

One of the main splashes of joy I receive when I go out to share my story is when women come up afterward and say, "Wow, after hearing YOUR story, I don't have any problems at ALL." Isn't it fabulous how God can take the fractured pieces of a life and use them to bless others? We trust that the stories in this book will brighten many dark corners and plant seeds of hope where there is defeat. There IS a door of hope, you know, and you not only can find that door, but you can walk confidently through it with a smile or even a chuckle when you get to the other side.

## Pain Can Isolate You

But finding others who can support you in your grief is not always easy, and sometimes you don't even want to find anyone, especially when tragedy first strikes. You can slip into such deep misery and depression, especially at the beginning, that you cut yourself off from all contacts. Pain can isolate you from friends, and even family, and that is exactly what happened to me. Right after learning about Larry, my heartache was so deep and so personal that I was unable to share it with others. I was just too sick and bruised, so I guarded my feelings and remained in my own prison of isolation.

I have heard of a method of prison-camp torture called "the cement sack." The cement sack is a concrete cubicle only big enough for a person to stand in during solitary confinement. In a real sense, I put myself in my own cement sack of anguish and misery. Misery is optional and at that time I chose misery of the worst kind.

After Bill would leave for work, I would stay alone in the back bedroom, counting the roses on the wallpaper and then breaking into periodic sobbing that sometimes took the form of wailing—the uttermost symbol of human agony. I had done a lot of crying over Steve and Tim, but the weeping I did over Larry was different. Normal crying is centered in the throat, but what I was doing came more out of my chest, where all the pain seemed to be located.

Without realizing it, I developed a "technique" to let out my grief. I now share this technique with others who are suffering this same kind of pain. I tell folks to lie across a pillow, face down (because this takes away restrictions in the chest and throat) and then let go—sob your heart out. In this position you can let the sobbing energy emerge more easily. Sobbing is as violent a release of physical energy as vomiting. Some parents who are in grief think that if they ever start this kind of sobbing, they won't be able to stop, but that is not true. When we realize that sobbing can be a tremendous release, and we know that our feelings are acceptable to God, we can channel our energy into getting rid of unresolved grief. Some psychologists suggest that grieving people *schedule* a sobbing time each day to help release their grief. Without knowing it, I suppose that was what I was doing before the "experts" discovered it.

While my periods of sobbing helped me release the huge reservoirs of pent-up grief, they did not prevent me from becoming depressed. Finally, Bill sent me to a psychologist who was of some help, but I continued in my depression because I couldn't apply what he was advising me to do. He tried to explain that he had had very little success in changing the orientation of homosexuals and that if Larry ever did contact me, I shouldn't try to talk to him about changing. I simply couldn't accept this idea. I knew that God could change all things, and I knew He could fix Larry if only I prayed hard enough.

My dialogue with the psychologist went on for months, but my depression grew worse. The day Dr. Wells told me that, because Larry had been gone almost a year, he might never come back, I went into such severe depression that he recommended to Bill that I be put in Parkside West, the psychiatric facility in our area.

Bill told Dr. Wells that he wasn't sure his insurance would cover me and, unless it did, we would tough it out at home, since I wasn't "really vicious or anything."

Just as the end of my rope was fraying, I learned one more key lesson about grief: I learned to REALLY let go, to relinquish the source of my grief TOTALLY to God.

That lesson came the next day, when I drove up to a high viaduct near Disneyland, planning to turn the wheel hard, go over the rail, and plunge fifty feet to what I hoped would be death. But as I neared the top, I realized two things:

1. Dropping fifty feet in a car might not do the whole job. I could wind up maimed, making baskets in the home for the bewildered.

2. I was TIRED. I was tired of the suffering and pain, tired of all the bittersweet memories, tired of the churning about Larry. Above all, I was tired of saying I was "giving him to God," but then in reality taking him back again and carrying the burden, myself. I was weary of being a shell of myself, unable to be rid of the heaviness in my heart.

It was then that I decided to "nail Larry to the Cross," and in my imagination, that's exactly what I did. I took out a hammer and I nailed him to the Cross as I prayed this prayer of relinquishment: "I can't handle this any more, Lord . . . I'm giving him to You, and if he never comes home and I never see him again, *whatever, Lord,* whatever happens, I'm nailing him to the Cross and giving him to You!"

I'm not really sure what happened or why, but I believe that the key words were, "Whatever, Lord." There was something about finally surrendering to God and telling Him that WHAT-EVER happened, whatever He decided to do or not do, it was all right with me. I was too tired to fight and struggle and churn any longer. I would accept whatever He chose to send my way.

When I said, "Whatever, Lord," it released a million little splashes of joy deep inside of me. My teeth stopped itching, the shag rug in my throat disappeared, the elephant that had been sitting on my chest for nearly a year was gone, and so was that knife twisting there close to my heart. I turned my car around and drove home to begin life again.

I realize that what happened for me is not necessarily what happens for everyone else. There is nothing magical or su-per-spiritual about saying "Whatever, Lord." The key, however, is to relinquish whatever is causing your pain. This is particularly true if it is a loved one who is leading a rebellious life. When I said, "Whatever, Lord," I was identifying with Job, who said, "Though He slay me, yet will I trust Him . . ." (Job 13:15, NKJV). Because I felt I had lost everything—except my mind, and that was slowly going, too—I came to the place where I could say, "Whatever, Lord," instead of, "Why me?"

That was the key. I personally surrendered my hopes . . . my plans . . . my life . . . MY SON. I realized I was powerless to fix him, to bring him back, or to change him. Only God's touch on Larry's life could do any of that. As Scripture says, God is the One who removes the heart of stone and puts a heart of flesh in its place.[3] I finally understood that all I could do was *let him go*—turn him over to God and let Him work in Larry's life.

## Try Giving Your Gift Box to Jesus

I am well aware that it may be hard to picture how you are to let go and give your child or other loved one to God. "Nailing him (or her) to the Cross" may not work for you as it worked for me that day I was on the verge of suicide. One way of looking at it is picturing in your mind that you are putting your loved one into a gift box. Then, in your mind's eye, wrap the box with lovely paper and ribbon.

Next, picture a long flight of stairs. At the top is the throne of God, with Jesus sitting on it. Imagine yourself climbing up these stairs, carrying your beautifully wrapped package. When you get to the top, put it at Jesus' feet and wait until He bends down to pick up the package and place it on His lap. Picture Jesus opening your package and taking your loved one in His arms to hold him or her close.

You must be sure that Jesus has your loved one in His grip, and you must believe that He will *never* let go. You have given your loved one to Jesus. He will take over. Now comes the crucial moment. When you've given your gift to Jesus, turn

around. Then walk back down the stairs. Halfway down, you may want to pause and see that your loved one is safe in Jesus' arms. You may want to hear in your mind's ear Jesus saying, "No one will ever take this precious one out of My hands and I will never let him go."

As you continue walking down the stairs, thank God for taking control. Then, hear yourself praying: *Lord, that settles it. I have given (name) to You and have taken my hands off. Do Your work in (his or her) life as you see fit.*

I believe this kind of exercise works with relinquishing any loved one, whether it is a child in open rebellion, someone who has made bad choices and mistakes, or someone who is a victim of a chronic disease or crippling injury. The point is, once you go through this mental exercise and pray this prayer, you do not have to feel as though everything now depends on you. Whenever you are tempted to take control again, you must practice this little thought exercise and remember that definite time when you presented your loved one as a gift to the Lord and He received him or her with His tender, everlasting love.

The simple sketch on page 60 could be copied and placed in a prominent place to continually remind you that you have given your loved one to God. He or she is safe in the arms of Jesus and you can go on about the tasks that Jesus wants you to do, instead of trying to carry burdens that are too big.

## Eternal Perspective Makes All the Difference

One reason I like the mental exercise of placing a loved one in Jesus' hands is that it focuses on the ETERNAL PERSPECTIVE that we need if we are to cope with disappointment and heartache. There is no better way out of the cesspool than the rope of eternal perspective—knowing that "THIS ISN'T IT." What is happening is only temporary, and it will pass. Having eternal perspective means keeping your rear-view mirror small and narrow and your windshield big and wide so that you can see farther down the road and look forward to what the future holds. True, you can't see the immediate future—tomorrow, next month, or even a few years from now. *But you do know you will be a winner in the end.*

I have never been much for the "name-it-and-claim-it" approach. Who really wants or needs this? Our eternal promise is so big and so glorious and full of blinding brightness that the dismal present fades in comparison. The present is a small glimpse of what life is really all about. The future is the big picture. And as we endure temporary heartaches, we will get a much clearer perception and realize:

THE IRON CROWN OF SUFFERING
PRECEDES THE GOLDEN CROWN OF GLORY.

Several years ago, my daughter-in-love, Shannon, drew a sketch like the one on page 58. Since that time, Bill has printed up thousands of these little sheets to be sent out to people served by Spatula Ministries. I tell the gals to put this little sign on their refrigerators or some other prominent place to remind them to always say, "WHATEVER, LORD!"

Since we started sending out these little signs, I've had about forty different women send me this same phrase done on glasses, napkins, and in needlepoint—just about any form you can think of. When I visit the homes of women who are part of our Spatula Ministries family, I often find the sheet tacked on their bulletin boards or framed and hanging on a wall.

## She Changed But Her Kid Didn't

Recently a lady came up to me after a conference and handed me an envelope with a note and a twenty-dollar bill inside. The note said:

When you were here around five years ago, my daughter had left her husband and two kids and declared she was a lesbian. You talked to me and gave me your book. I was to send you the money for it.

Out of anger, because my daughter didn't change, I didn't send it. My daughter still hasn't changed, but I have. I've given it all to God and left it there. Here is the money for the book.

Love in Christ,
Sally

I love this lady's letter, not because she finally paid for the book, but because she saw that it is *our* job to love folks and it is *God's* job to change them. Parents naturally want to bring about immediate changes in their kids' lives, but God didn't command us to change them., He only commanded us to LOVE them. It is God who makes the changes in ANY of us.

Lots of parents have what some psychologists call the "rescue fantasy." They want to rearrange their children's lives and provide the happy ending, but that is not what God has told us to do. The very best we can do, other than listening to hurting folks and weeping with them, is to point to the only One who can really help bring healing. I often tell parents to remember to say:

I DIDN'T CAUSE IT,
I CANNOT CONTROL IT,
NOR CAN I CURE IT.

But God can! We have two choices when we are faced with suffering and tragedy: We can withdraw and become bitter, growing old before our time and dying inwardly, or we can reach out to God and grow inwardly. We have God's promise that it will happen and "there hath not failed one word of all His good promise . . ." (1 Kings 8:56, KJV).

## Love Is the Glue That Mends Broken Hearts

The road to recovery is not a straight, upward climb. But you begin by realizing that you must understand that *it is not always necessary to understand everything.* Sometimes it will be a case of three steps forward and one step back. Or sometimes hope will reign in the morning only to be overcome by despair before sundown. Various emotions, like anger, depression, longing, and bitterness may chase each other through your mind, making it impossible to think logically or make sound decisions.

Each day becomes a new challenge to live without dropping back into that cesspool of shocked helplessness. You can be at peace for a few days and then suddenly the loneliness and emptiness will come rushing back. Perhaps you will look at the calendar and see that it is the birthday of your wayward daughter. Or perhaps you will see someone on the street who strongly resembles the child over whom you are grieving. That happened with me. I would be in a shopping mall and see a young man in the distance who had on a sport shirt exactly like one Larry owned. Just seeing that shirt would send waves of heartache through me. My strength would evaporate, and for the moment I would be defeated and dissolve in tears.

Sometimes your recovery period will be like a roller coaster with many highs and lows. At times you'll want to scream because you think the bottom is dropping out, that the heart-stopping plunge will never end, that you are totally out of control. But then you will feel the pain subsiding and the wound will start to heal and life will become a bit brighter because now you have a glimmer of hope. And once you have THAT, you are on your way, because hope is tough to kill.

As the saying goes, "Hope springs eternal." We hope even when all hope is supposed to be gone. We hope long after everyone else has given up. Hope can live with virtually no reinforcement. Hope can mend your broken heart—if you give God ALL the pieces.

We can face whatever comes once we have relinquished our lives and the lives of our loved ones to Him. He is the God we can trust for strength each day (see Deut. 33:25). He is the One with all the love and understanding, who has a clear and eternal purpose for us. We can trust God with all our problems, all our heartaches, and especially with all our long-term anxieties. Every morning as we wake ourselves up with a splash of joy we can say, "WHATEVER, LORD!"

**Splish/Splash . . .**

THE RAIN FALLS ON THE JUST AND ALSO ON THE UNJUST,
BUT CHIEFLY ON THE JUST,
BECAUSE THE UNJUST STEALS THE JUST'S UMBRELLA.

\* \* \* \* \* \*

CHANGE IS A PROCESS, NOT AN EVENT.

\* \* \* \* \* \*

WE ARE ALWAYS IN THE FORGE, OR ON THE ANVIL;
BY TRIALS GOD IS SHAPING US FOR HIGHER THINGS.

\* \* \* \* \* \*

WHATEVER YOU WANT, LORD . . .

W — Whoever You put in, or take out of my life . . .
H — However You want things to end up . . . only You see the big picture.
A — As much as I can take, Lord . . . You know me best because
T — Time is nothing to You . . . help me to be patient.
E — Everything is in Your hands . . . Help me to let go.
V — Victory comes with You as my Guide.
E — Eternity with You will be worth it all!
R — Restoration is mine through You.

\* \* \* \* \* \*

Take Your Broken Dreams to Jesus!

The Lord lifts the fallen and those bent beneath their loads.
(Ps. 145:14, TLB)

# Wherever I Go, There I Am

*If I have inside of me the stuff to make cocoons, maybe
the stuff of butterflies is there, too.*

Trina Paulus[1]

There's something about falling into a cesspool that just doesn't do much to improve your self-image. When disappointment and rejection invade our lives, they often rob us of our self-esteem as well. Many folks write to tell me what it's like to have your self-esteem flushed right down the toilet. They seldom use the terms "self-image" and "self-esteem," but that's what their letters are telling us.

One mother of an adult daughter and son wrote to say that first her daughter proclaimed her homosexuality by moving in with a woman friend who had a little boy. Neither this mother or her husband could accept their daughter's choice of lifestyle and they wrote letters to tell her they loved her and she would always be welcome in their home, but the rest of her "family" would not. The daughter responded by saying she appreciated the letters, but that she would not be seeing much of her parents and regretted that they would miss out on enjoying her family, especially the

67

new "grandson." And no, she would not be home for Christmas.

Sensing a certain reserve in their son, they asked him what he thought of his sister's decision. That's when he told them that he, too, was gay. The mother's letter said, in part:

> Barbara, *I do want to resign as a mother.* I am ready to go be with Jesus. I DON'T WANT MY ONLY SON AND MY ONLY DAUGHTER TO BE GAY! . . . I want to have grandchildren; I want us to be a "normal" American family. I don't want this guilt, pain, shame and heartache. I don't want this little town to whisper and gossip about my children. I don't want my husband's eyes to flash pain and guilt when he is trying to be strong for me. . . .
>
> People have often counted on my faith, my interest and caring and yes—good spirits—to help them. I am a piano and voice teacher, and my 40 students are friends as well as students. Now I feel like a "zombie" in the studio. I sing in the choir and as a soloist in other groups. I feel like a fraud . . . I am 54 and I wonder what it was all for. What did my life accomplish? I have never felt so worthless or helpless.

Another mother, from Arizona, wrote to say it had been over a year since their youngest daughter's letter had arrived, announcing, "What I need to tell you is that I am a lesbian. There it is. Now where do I go from here?" The mother's letter continued:

> Our lives will never be the same. I feel I lost self-esteem and have to work to overcome this feeling of being lethargic. I am on an antidepressant, but it's a constant struggle to get work done.

That feeling of lethargy also overwhelms a woman who is a columnist for her local newspaper. Her husband had died and she had also lost a sister who had suffered painfully with Alzheimer's disease for eighteen years. Then a son was divorced and his two children suffered horribly from the results. Her letter said:

I used to speak to women on beauty and how to bring out your best. I need to do something, but my batteries are dead. I wail. Pray. Feel totally alone. I have no immediate family. Friends—yes—but still s-o-o-o alone.

Where do I go from here? I am a writer. My columns help people, but nothing is helping me.

Letters like these aren't unusual; they are typical of so many that come in all the time. When your self-esteem lies in tatters, you feel like saying:

> I USED TO BE APATHETIC.
> NOW I JUST DON'T CARE!

## Self-Esteem Is Like a Three-Legged Stool

We all have a mental picture of ourselves. That picture is our self-image, and we will act in harmony with what we see in that mental self-portrait.[2] Another way to describe self-esteem is that it is simply how you feel about yourself. Do you like or dislike yourself? So much of the grief I hear about is the kind that can make a person dislike herself. It can make her feel worthless, helpless, and cut adrift, belonging nowhere.

A helpful way to look at what your self-esteem does for you is to picture a three-legged stool, with each leg representing a major feeling you have about yourself:

1. I belong.
2. I am worthwhile.
3. I am capable.[3]

*To belong is to feel wanted, loved, cared for, accepted.* One woman wrote to me to tell me what it feels like *not* to belong:

> I'm 40 years old, with nine kids. My husband ran off with another woman four years ago when I was one month pregnant with my three-year-old *twins*. I've got no emotional support from my family . . . my older children avoid me because I suffer from panic attacks. I can't drive my car. I don't leave my

home because I'm afraid I will have a panic attack and can't get back.

They think I've already lost my mind, but I know if I don't get some help soon I <u>will</u> lose my mind.

HELP!

Most of us have felt like this gal at some time or another. When I first learned that homosexuality was part of our family, I felt like an alien from another planet. I could not relate to anyone, and no one was relating to me. My feelings of self-worth were totally squashed. But there have been other times, maybe not so serious and occasionally even comical, when my self-esteem has been bruised more than a little bit.

When my first book, *Where Does a Mother Go to Resign?* came out, I was totally unfamiliar with being an author. I really didn't know what to do when folks would come up, hug me, thank me, and ask me to sign their book with "something just for them." Was I supposed to put in a Bible verse or just their name and my name? Was I supposed to add some spiritual thoughts? Being an author left me a little bewildered.

The book had been out only a few weeks when I stopped at a huge Christian bookstore in Orange County, California to make several purchases. As I looked through different books, I noticed that the authors had signed them on the flyleaf. Since so many authors live in the Orange County area, I assumed that when they had visited that store, they had just signed their own books so buyers could have a personally autographed copy.

Then I came upon a big stack of MY book, all lined up on a rack marked "New Books Just Published." I took out my handy pen and started writing my name in the flyleaf of the books. As I happily signed my name, I just relished the idea of thinking how surprised buyers would be to buy the book and then discover it had already been autographed!

Suddenly, a tall, serious-looking young man put his hand on my shoulder and said in a stern voice, "Lady, we don't allow people to deface our books here!"

I looked at the young man and thought of how I could respond. Should I get out my driver's license to prove who I was? Should I just scribble all over one of the books in defiance? Or maybe I would just slink out without a word of explanation. I felt so unworthy at that moment. After all, the book was just off the press, and if I had a big altercation with a Christian bookstore over "defacing" its merchandise, where would it all end?

I decided to just get out of there, and I did so without telling the young man who I was. I guess I thought that would only make it worse! Anyway, I knew I didn't belong there at that moment because I just wasn't ACCEPTABLE.

*To feel worthwhile, or worthy, is to feel that you count,* that you are doing the right thing, not the wrong thing, that you are a good person, not a bad one. One gal's letter describes what it's like to be made to feel worthless:

> As a family with a homosexual daughter, we have had a flood of emotions. . . . We live in a small farming community

where there are three churches and everyone knows everyone else's business. In fact, everyone is just about related one
way or another. I suppose you can guess what happened
when we found out that Cindy was living a homosexual
lifestyle!

We had an evangelist in our church and he made this statement: "Any time a child becomes a homosexual, let me repeat,
ANYTIME, whether male or female, it is ALWAYS the fault of
the mother." This is just what I needed, on top of everything
else.

The evangelist's unfortunate (and totally untrue) words did
this mom untold damage. I wrote back and told her that her
daughter's problem was NOT HER FAULT. One of my biggest tasks is to assure parents that when their children have a
problem or decide to go astray, they do not have to feel guilty.
(I'll say more on this in chapter 8.)

*And to feel capable means that you know you can do it—* you're
up to whatever life may bring. You know you have the strength.
You have confidence. A mother, whose son appears to have
"married" his gay lover and now wears a ring in his nose as
well as several in his ear, wrote to tell me her world was crum-
bling and everything was out of control:

> I don't think it could hurt any worse if he put on spike shoes
> and ground me into the ground—or put a knife in me and
> twisted it. . . . Barbara, please say something to help me get a
> grip on things again. I thought I was doing well and was help-
> ing others in the same situation. But now I feel I am sinking
> again.

My counsel to this mother was that, while her son was not
behaving like an adult, he still was one and he had to make his
own choices. As parents, we cannot always change the behavior of our kids, especially when they're adults. Also, we cannot
let the sin of one child disturb the entire family. Her son had
made some bad choices, but WHEN THERE IS NO CONTROL,
THERE IS NO RESPONSIBILITY. She was not to blame for her

son's behavior; what she needed to do was resist sliding back down into a cesspool of defeat.

I prayed with this mom and we asked God to help her get through this temporary setback. Now she was off balance and deeply hurt, but she would get through it. She wouldn't always feel this way if she would only hang on to that "rope of hope."

I believe that in cases like this there is a phrase that applies:

HURT PEOPLE HURT PEOPLE.

This mother's son was hurting inside, and he was striking out, wanting to hurt someone else, which is typical. If we remember that people who are hurt often strike out, in turn, to hurt others, it will help us to show compassion. Condemnation will not work. The only way anyone changes is through conviction, which comes from inside.

## Think Highly of Yourself—But Not Too Highly

One of the best verses I've ever seen on self-esteem is Romans 12:3 (NIV): "Do not think of yourself more highly than you ought, but rather think of yourself with sober judgment, in accordance with the measure of faith God has given you." Some Christians believe this verse says we should not be concerned about high self-esteem, that we shouldn't think highly of ourselves at all, that we should put ourselves down to be lowly and humble enough for Jesus to accept us. But if we look again at Romans 12:3, we see that it does *not* say, "Never think highly of yourself—that's sinful." What it *does* say is, "Think highly of yourself—have self-respect—but don't get conceited or egotistical."

As Josh McDowell puts it, "In other words, we should be realistic and biblical in our opinions of ourselves. . . . We are to

develop a healthy self-image, or self-evaluation that coincides
with what God says about us. . . ." He continues:

A HEALTHY SELF-IMAGE IS SEEING YOURSELF
AS GOD SEES YOU—NO MORE AND NO LESS.[4]

So, no matter what has happened, no matter how badly one
of your children has strayed or rebelled, no matter how badly
your spouse or other family members or friends have treated
you, you are *still God's child*, made in His image and *very precious* to Him. You are a son or daughter of the King—you are
royalty. Someone sent in the following poem, which says it very
well:

> When the *child* of God
> Looks into the *Word* of God
> And sees the *Son* of God
> He is *changed* by the *Spirit* of God
> In the *image* of God
> For the *glory* of God.

One of my favorite bumper "snickers" says, "Life is hard
and then you die." Actually, that's the GOOD news because
when Christians die, life's struggles are over and we go to be
with the Lord. But the reason so many people have low (unhealthy) self-esteem is that "life is hard and you have to live it
anyway." As Ashleigh Brilliant says,

IT'S EASY TO COME AND GO;
THE HARD THING IS TO REMAIN.[5]

But remaining is what life is all about. And you'll never
raise your self-image if you blame circumstances or other
people for your feelings. For example, some of us blame
our low self-images on our parents, and it's true that mothers and fathers can do more to destroy (or build) a child's
self-esteem than anyone. My husband, Bill, knows something about that.

## Bill Became an Ace Anyhow

Bill and I went to a communication seminar given by Norman Wright a few years ago and one of our assignments was, "Write down something you remember that your father said to praise you or a good thing he said about you."

I dashed off several memories I had of when my dad had encouraged me, but Bill sat there with nothing on his page. I knew what he was thinking. He had come from a very rigid family and was the only child. His father, particularly, never showed much emotion or did anything to encourage him.

When World War II hit, Bill went into the navy to become a flier. His father told him he would NEVER make it in the navy as a flier, but Bill made it and then some. During the war, he became an "ace." According to government policy, an ace is any flier who shoots down more than six enemy planes, and Bill shot down seven. He was decorated with the Distinguished Flying Cross twice. He also was awarded two air medals, the Purple Heart, and the Presidential Unit Citation for Bravery.

In spite of all the achievements and honors Bill won, not once did his father ever admit he was wrong about his son or even congratulate him for his admirable record as a U.S. Navy flier.

So it was no wonder that Bill had to sit and think for several minutes before coming up with something his father had ever said to fill his emotional tank. Finally, just before we were to begin discussing what we all had written, Bill put this down:

> One time when I was about five, I was riding in the backseat of the car and my father and my uncle were in the front. My uncle's hat flew out of the open window and he turned around and started blaming me for tossing out his hat. But my father said, "Billy didn't throw your hat out the window."

This was the ONLY thing Bill could remember that his father had ever said to defend him or say anything remotely positive about him. But the good thing about all this is that, despite never getting any encouragement from his father, Bill didn't let that defeat him. He didn't allow that to destroy his self-esteem. He went on and made a tremendous success of his life. Somehow he knew he was worthwhile and capable. That made it possible for him to succeed.

The truth is, each one of us is special—a unique product made by God, and, as the well-known saying goes:

GOD DON'T MAKE NO JUNK.

## He Isn't Finished with Any of Us Yet

God not only made you special, He's still working on you and in you to will and to do His good pleasure. He isn't finished with you yet.

When my son, Larry, was in college, a teacher gave his psychology class the following assignment: "Stand nude before a full-length mirror. Make a self-evaluation of what is seen."

In response, Larry turned in an essay that said, in part:

This particular assignment created a problem for me. To submit myself to this assignment would violate my own personal convictions. I have dedicated my body to the Lord Jesus Christ and upon doing this am unable to follow the exact assignment. I have kept in mind your goal of self-evaluation and would like to share what I have learned about myself. . . .

I consider God as my maker. He is the artist working on my life, and is more concerned with my inward qualities, building into me an enduring structure. Others are passers-by who do not realize the intentions or abilities of the Creator in my life's pattern. Therefore, it is not my place to judge God's unfinished work because of one very vital fact, GOD IS NOT FINISHED WITH ME YET!

It is one thing to be descriptive, another to be judgmental. I feel the information you asked for would be both. In describ-

ing myself as assigned, I would be using others' standards as
to my height, bulkiness, and conformation. . . .

I have found that I form a NEGATIVE self-image by accepting the values of people around me, but a POSITIVE and accu-
rate self-image develops when I comprehend the values which
God places on my appearance, abilities, parentage, and environment. Opinions of others create inferiority, insecurity, and
rejection. However, because I have confidence in God's principles and design, I understand and joyfully accept the values
He places on my life, because I can see what can happen to a
vessel God is shaping for His own use. . . .

You asked me to tell you what was done to discover myself.
I did two things. I began with a personal relationship with God.
I accepted His plan and purpose for my life. I let God take charge
of the design, and thanked Him for His workmanship thus far.
I realized that God was not finished with me yet, and I began
to have a new confidence and expectation for what He will do
for the future.

Now I can thank God for His constant love toward me, and
His Son who died for me that I may live—and mostly for the
knowledge that my life is being constantly molded by Him into
an object of use. God is the potter and I am the clay. I am the
product of His design and my life reflects His workmanship
and HE IS NOT FINISHED WITH ME YET.

## We're All on the Same Road

Even though he didn't complete the assignment as given,
Larry still got a good grade on his paper. Perhaps his teacher
realized that what Larry said about himself is true of all of us.
God isn't finished with any of us yet. Yes, there is changing
and shaping that He wants to do, but He does it because we
belong to Him, we are of infinite worth to Him, and He sees
tremendous potential in what we can do.

On a trip I made to Texas, Kentucky, and the state of Washington, it was terrific to meet so many gals who have become
part of Spatula Ministries. Once again, I realized how we are
all bonded together by heartaches and how God's love brings

us the healing touch, drains the pain, and helps us move along on the road to becoming well.

While on that trip, I was on highway 395 in Spokane. I knew Barney and his family live in their new home on highway 395 in Nevada, several hundred miles south of where I was. I telephoned Barney and when he answered I said, "I'm up here on highway 395—we're both on the same road."

Barney laughed and said, "That's right. Only you're just a lot farther north—closer to heaven maybe?"

We had a good visit and some more laughs, and then I began thinking that this is really how life is. We are ALL on the same road. Some of us are just not where we were. We have moved on and have come through the rough places—"farther along," as the old song goes. We've all been brought together by God's redeeming love to be forgiven for our mistakes, cleansed, and then sent on down the road, sharing together as we go.

That's a splash of joy that should build anyone's self-esteem, but, as somebody said,

> THERE'S NOTHING LIKE A LITTLE EXPERIENCE
> TO UPSET A THEORY.

It's all very well and good to know you're on the same road with everyone else, but what about feeling as if you've just been run over? Beautiful, capable, never-have-a-thing-go-wrong people have a way of doing that without even meaning to. Maybe, like me, you identify with the unknown woman who wrote the following:

### HAVING A HARD DAY?

When I read about a woman who's totally together careerwise, I'm proud—and I go home and eat a carton of Cool Whip.

When I read about a woman who has a perfect relationship with a supportive, sensitive man—I go home and eat a carton of Cool Whip and scream.

When I read about a woman who has adorable, bilingual children and regular, open, loving chats with her mother—I write out my frustrations in M&Ms and eat them one paragraph at a time. This Ideal Woman seems too far out of reach; it's hopeless.

It may not be realistic to try to match some "ideal woman" who has gifts that you do not. (She also may have her own problems—far worse than yours!) What you want to do is develop your own potential while you let God do His work in you. Actually, you and God are a team. As Paul opened his letter to the Philippian church, he said, "I am sure that God who began the good work within you will keep right on helping you grow in his grace until his task within you is finally finished . . ." (Phil. 1:6, TLB).

Then Paul went on to say, "Continue to work out your salvation with fear and trembling, for it is God who works in you to will and to act according to his good purpose (Phil. 2:12, 13, NIV).

This verse is the key to healthy (not egotistical) self-esteem. Paul is saying we must make ourselves available instead of shrinking back or becoming a recluse as I did for almost a year when our son, Larry, walked out of our lives to pursue a gay lifestyle. When I finally told God, "Whatever, Lord!" I not only released Larry completely to Him, I also released the lonely burden I had been carrying all by myself all that time. I sang all the way home that day. It was the first time since Larry had gone that I felt assurance that God still loved me.

## We Are Opals, Not Diamonds

"She's a diamond in the rough" is a familiar way of saying somebody has potential to become far more than she is right now. But I believe that we are much more like opals than diamonds. Did you know that an opal is made of desert dust, sand, and silica and owes its beauty not to its perfection but to a defect? The opal is a stone with a broken heart. It is full of minute fissures that allow air inside, and then the air refracts the light. As a result, the opal has such lovely hues that the stone is called "the lamp of fire" because the breath of the Lord is in it.

An opal will lose its luster if it is kept in a cold, dark place, but the luster is restored when it is held in a warm hand or when light shines on it.

In so many ways, we can compare the opal to ourselves. It is when we are warmed by God's love that we take on color and brilliance. It is when we are broken inside ourselves—through our defects—that we can give back the lovely hues of His light to others. It is then that the lamp of the temple can burn brightly within us and not flicker or go out.

Still, there will be times when we lose the luster in our lives and it is vital to know how to restore it. When silver or brass become tarnished, we get out the tarnish remover and do some rubbing. What can we do when we need to bring back the shine in our own lives? We can pause early in the day to seek God's guidance. We can count our blessings and name them one by one.

An attitude of gratitude rids our lives of the film of frustration, the rust of resentment, and the varnish of vanity—all destroyers of self-esteem. When we count our blessings, we multiply harmony and good feelings, and the lamp's flame burns higher once again.

Without God's touch in our lives—His work in us to will and to do His good pleasure—there is no sparkle or scant joy. But when we allow Him to work within us—when we feel His hand upon us—we are no longer hidden treasures; we become sparkling jewels that beautify His kingdom.


## Up, Up, and Away!

It's easy to talk about having a good self-esteem when life is soaking you with plenty of splashes of joy, but when you are in the cesspool of low self-esteem, it's different. I've been there and I know. Getting out of that cesspool seems impossible. The sides seem too "slickery" and slimy. But you can do it if you are willing to try and at the same time have faith that God is doing His work in you. Here are some ideas that can pull you up, out of the cesspool. They are simple ideas, but they are like ropes to help you climb up the slippery sides and make it back to seeing yourself as God sees you, no more and no less.

**There is always something new you can learn.** I'm not talking about nuclear physics or computer science (unless that's what you really want to do). I'm talking about simpler things, like learning new words or maybe reading up on faraway exotic places. Because I travel a lot, I like looking for unusual names of towns across the country. Lately I've developed my own "Joy Map" of the United States, which shows only the names of towns that are positive, fun, and uplifting. I'll tell you more about that in chapter 7.

The point is, the better informed you are, the more vital you will be, not only to others but to yourself. And as you become more aware of others, your self-esteem is bound to rise.

**Learn what builds your confidence and take advantage of it.** Remember one of the three legs of self-esteem? It's the idea that "I am capable—I can handle this."

You can find confidence in strange places—at the cosmetic counter with a new shade of mascara or lipstick, at the beauty parlor with a new hairdo or permanent, or at the clothing store where you can find a new dress or sweater.

Sometimes, when I feel a need for an injection of confidence, I pull out an old shoebox that I have kept for years. It is my original "Joy Box" and inside it are notes, letters, and greeting cards sent by special friends, some of whom have gone on to Glory. Every time I read through the cards and letters I get a lift. It is as if my special friends are talking to me. We all need others who can nurture us, enrich us, and remind us that we are valuable to them as friends, too.

I call my several special friends my "nurturing ones." Everybody should have four or five nurturers they can call. As you share with them, you can tell from their very tone of voice that you are being cared for, that your life is being enriched. It may be their gentle laughter or some subtle way of reminding you how much they care. A phone call to one of my special nurturing ones restores my confidence as much as anything I know.

**Spend your time with others who pick you up and don't put you down.** Find friends who accept you for who you are, instead of cutting you down to size to make themselves feel larger. If your spouse or your children put you down, let them know firmly but lovingly that you won't accept it. If your mother (or mother-in-law) is driving you toward the home for the bewildered, spend reasonable amounts of time with her, but don't let her control your life.

**Emphasize your strengths and stay away from your weaknesses.** Everybody does something well, even if it's as simple as crossword puzzles, Scrabble, or tying a scarf with just the right touch. If Mother Nature cheated you in certain parts of the looks department, emphasize the things that she did a better job on. It might be your hair, your eyes, your smile, or your ability to be kind and caring. Develop your specialty and use it every day. As you concentrate on your strengths you will have less time to dwell on your weaknesses.

One of the strengths I've developed is interviewing folks, which is a skill I didn't have some years ago when I began working as an intake receptionist at a counseling center. My responsibility was to interview potential counselees on the phone and make arrangements for their stay at the counseling center, which sometimes would last for many weeks. I would take down their histories and ascertain what crises they were in, how immediate their need might be, and if a spouse or other companion should accompany them.

One day a man called and sounded very disturbed, saying he wanted to bring his wife in for counseling right away. As I began to get the facts from him, he excitedly told me how impossible his wife was to reason with. When she had refused his suggestions to get help, he had shaved her head completely BALD! My shock was so great that I couldn't help muttering, "Well, we sure won't have any difficulty in recognizing HER, will we?"

It has taken time, but since that day I have learned to be more diplomatic. Now I really enjoy talking with people, drawing them out, and letting them share their feelings with me. All of which gives me good feelings about myself, as well.

### The "I Am's" Are the Real You

One other thing you can do to build healthy self-esteem is become a student of what the Bible says about you. The following is a list of "I am" verses. Study one every day for two weeks and when you get through with the list, start over again—or find others! Soon these verses will become part of your very being, part of who you think you are and who you see when you gaze into the mirror:

I AM . . .

1. A child of God (Rom. 8:16).
2. Forgiven (Col. 1:13, 14).
3. Saved by grace through faith (Eph. 2:8).
4. Justified (Rom. 5:1).
5. A new creature (2 Cor. 5:17).
6. Led by the Spirit of God (Rom. 8:14).
7. Kept in safety wherever I go (Ps. 91:11).
8. Casting all my cares on Jesus (1 Pet. 5:7).
9. Doing all things through Christ who strengthens me (Phil. 4:13).
10. Bringing every thought into captivity (2 Cor. 10:5).
11. Being transformed by a renewed mind (Rom. 12:1, 2).
12. The righteousness of God in Christ (2 Cor. 5:21).
13. An imitator of Jesus (Eph. 5:1).
14. Filled with laughter and rejoicing (Job 8:21).

Recently I was at the NBC studios in Burbank, California to tape a television show on the role of women in today's society. I was escorted to the makeup room and left there alone for a few minutes. I sat in the makeup chair looking at a big mirror surrounded by those bright, merciless lights. All around the room were photos of movie stars of today and yesterday—Lana Turner, Ann Sheridan, Rita Hayworth, Loretta Young, and dozens more. But the focal point of the whole scene was the sign placed just above the mirror, which proclaimed in huge black letters:

IF YOU WANT MAKE-UP, ASK ME.
IF YOU WANT MIRACLES, ASK GOD.

When you're looking in the mirror at a time like that, it's always good to remember some of the "I am" verses.

**Take a Risk—and Be Free!**

Also remember that the key to climbing out of that cesspool of low self-esteem is willingness to take a risk. Actually, you *can* stay down in the cesspool and not take any risks at all. It's safer there, even if it isn't a pleasant place to be. On the other hand, you can dare to make things different. As Helen Keller said:

LIFE IS EITHER A DARING ADVENTURE
OR NOTHING.

I got a letter recently from a woman who has had all kinds of trouble with her sons who are now twenty-two and twenty years old. One of them left home when he was fourteen. She didn't hear from him for eight years and then received a call that he was in prison doing a twenty-five-year sentence for armed robbery. The other son is an alcoholic who has left his job, home, and belongings and has disappeared. A warrant has been issued for his arrest. In spite of all these cesspools, this mother writes:

> The years of my life have been miserable and self-defeating. But beneath it all I knew God was in charge and everything would ultimately be okay. Not pie in the sky, just simple truth. Because I grew up abused, I've had little self-esteem until these past three or four years. I have joy in me, and even in bitter times I could see humor and joy, but some around me thought me strange for that. With no personal strength (how could I be strong without the freedom of Jesus?) it added to my belief of being a wrong, weird person. But now I am free! How glorious to stand in the light, how safe. When I am afraid, I take slow, deep breaths and say, "I am safe in Jesus."

This mom has learned a crucial secret to preserving her tattered self-esteem:

PICK UP THE PIECES AND GO ON.

You can do this in all kinds of situations: when real tragedy strikes or in lighter moments, when you need to turn a minor disaster into a serendipity. I was speaking for a large women's group at a big hotel in Texas, and it seemed that problems were coming from every direction. The adjoining room had a banquet going on with lots of singing and loud music with drums. The microphone I was using kept cutting out every now and then, and to add to the problem, the air conditioning was inadequate for such a large room. To top it off, the chairs were the kind you could sit in for only twenty-five minutes without wanting to escape.

As I tried to compete with the loud music and the microphone malfunction, I hurried through my story in half the time it usually takes and had to leave out many of the details that would normally pull it all together.

Afterward, I made my way to the powder room and, while I was using the facilities, three gals who had heard my talk came bursting in. They were just bubbling over with words like, "Oh, wasn't that GREAT!" "Did you ever laugh and cry at the same time and feel so GOOD about it?" "Boy, I sure wouldn't have missed today for ANYTHING! I haven't been so encouraged and blessed in ages!"

I wanted to come out and hug all three of them, but instead I decided it would be best to remain unseen until they left. They would never know how their words had buoyed me up. Proverbs says, "Anxious hearts are very heavy but a word of encouragement does wonders!"[6] How true, especially when it is an OVERHEARD word, which really wasn't meant for your ears!

I felt renewed. I felt restored. My trip had been worthwhile after all because some people—at least three of them, anyway—were helped and refreshed. And in return, their encouraging words had glued together my broken pieces and I could go on.

That's always the key—*pick up the pieces and keep going*, even when it seems that the whole world is against you. It really isn't, you know. As one psychiatrist said to his patient: "The whole world isn't against you; there are millions of people who don't care one way or another."

But those who really love you care. And above all, God cares. We all have fractures in our lives. Sometimes they are physical, sometimes emotional, and sometimes mental. But we know that God can heal those fractured places, and He can glue together the fragments that are cracked and split and make us whole. Knowing that He cares is the secret of good self-esteem—seeing yourself as God sees you, no more and no less.


**Splish/Splash . . .**

SOME THINGS NEVER CHANGE . . .
LIKE THE TASTE OF POSTAGE-STAMP GLUE.

*     *     *     *     *     *

### BE GOOD TO YOU

Be yourself—truthfully.
Accept yourself—gratefully.
Value yourself—joyfully.
Forgive yourself—completely.
Treat yourself—generously.
Balance yourself—harmoniously.
Bless yourself—abundantly.
Trust yourself—confidently.
Love yourself—wholeheartedly.
Empower yourself—prayerfully.
Give yourself—enthusiastically.
Express yourself—radiantly.

Source unknown

\*    \*    \*    \*    \*    \*

MOST PEOPLE ARE WILLING TO CHANGE,
NOT BECAUSE THEY SEE THE LIGHT,
BUT BECAUSE THEY FEEL THE HEAT!

\*    \*    \*    \*    \*    \*

Dear Christ, I would give
You every key of the little house that
You know as me.
The porch has been Yours,
And You've walked all through
The open rooms that the world can view.
But today, O Christ, I would have You go
To the secret rooms that I've treasured so.
They are hidden and small and set apart;
But I want You to own this house—my heart.

Source unknown

\*    \*    \*    \*    \*    \*

HAVE CHARACTER!
Don't BE one!

\*   \*   \*   \*   \*   \*

CHEER UP!
TOMORROW WILL BE DIFFERENT . . .
NOT BETTER, JUST DIFFERENT!

\*   \*   \*   \*   \*   \*

But why is man important to you?
  Why do you take care of human beings?
You made man a littler lower than the angels.
  And You crowned him with glory and honor.
                                   Ps. 8:4, 5, NCV

# S.D.D.D.D.
## *(Same Doo-Doo, Different Day)*

*Don't lose your head in the battle . . . you won't have
any place to put your helmet.*

A recurring theme in many of the letters I receive is STRESS, the
daily wear and tear that comes from just being alive. I love the
quip about the lady who goes for a drive whenever things get
too stressful—she is now twenty-six hundred miles from home.

One thing my mail reminds me of is that we all have different lives, different cesspools, and different kinds of stress. A
reader in the Northwest wrote this candid response after reading *So, Stick a Geranium in Your Hat and Be Happy*:

> I am sorry that your two older sons were killed. I can only
> imagine how difficult that must be. I pray that I never have to
> know that particular anguish.
>
> However, I must take issue with your reaction when you
> found out that your third son was a homosexual. My first reac-
> tion was "Lighten up, Lady!" That's basically how I felt after
> finishing the book, too.
>
> So your son is gay. Big deal. Has he robbed anybody? My
> son has. Has he been arrested for breaking and entering? My

son has. Has he been on drugs and/or alcohol? My son has. Has he killed anybody? My son has. An accident, but the boy is still dead, and my son went to jail for it. All this before he was 17.

This woman went on to talk a little about the stress she's been experiencing the last two years. Her husband was diagnosed with renal-cell cancer, which had also spread to his lungs. Then their fourteen-year-old daughter told them she was pregnant and wanted to place the baby for adoption.

Later in the fall, her husband had his left kidney removed, and their son, who had been paroled to a state group home,

lost his job. When her husband was in the hospital for his operation, she had to drive 150 miles each way to see him. Later, when he was able to go back to work, they both had to drive 100 miles round trip to work each day to their jobs.

Their son found another job, but then lost it and moved home with them, where his car was stolen and wrecked, and then he wrecked a replacement his parents bought for him. He also ran up $850 on their gasoline credit card in one month. On the good-news side, the treatment for her husband's cancer "seemed to be working," her daughter's baby was born, and her son got another job. But the stress continued; she wrote:

> My dear, *that* was stress. Stress is also having the doctor tell you that if the experimental treatment for cancer that your husband is undergoing doesn't work, there is nothing else to try. Stress is having your 20-year-old son call you in the middle of the night because he's out of work and out of money. Stress is facing the possibility of going on alone without enough money to meet the bills. Stress is not having enough to pay the bills, even after Don is home and back to work. Stress is seeing your first grandchild once for two minutes, and being afraid to hold him for fear you wouldn't be able to let go.

I appreciate this gal's letter because she tells it like it is. I called her to say that I understood and we had a good talk. She says things are better now, but her stress goes on. That's what causes the wear and tear, the constant, never-ending crises. As somebody said,

> THESE DAYS
> IT TAKES NERVES OF STEEL
> JUST TO BE NEUROTIC.

Every day we live out the proof that stress is HERE, a fact of life, and we must learn to cope with it. You may have seen the cartoon that shows Ziggy driving by a highway sign reading:

HARSH REALITIES NEXT 2,500 MILES.

Actually, the harsh realities last a lot longer than that. The sign could read:

HARSH REALITIES FOR THE REST OF THE TRIP.

## How Do You Handle Stress?

Karol Jackowski, author of *Ten Fun Things to Do Before You Die*, suggests that taking a long, hot-tub bubble bath is a great way to escape reality. She writes: "Because we are not God, the more we exceed our limits, the more we need to escape. Too much limitlessness is plain too much: overwhelming overload. Enough is enough is enough. No one knows better than you when you've reached or gone past your limit. So, when enough is definitely enough, find a place to escape reality and don't come back until you have to."[1]

I like what this poem has to say about reality and stress:

WHY ESCAPE?

Reality is the leading
cause of stress amongst
those in touch with it.
I can take it in small doses, but
as a lifestyle I found it too confining.
It was just too needful;
it expected me to be there for it
all the time,
and with all I have to do—
I had to let something go.
Now,
since I put reality on a back burner,
my days are jam-packed
and
fun-filled.
Jane Wagner[2]

## Two Main Approaches to Stress

Readers of our *Love Line* newsletter and other folks who hear me speak constantly send me ideas that work for them when handling stress. As I sort through them all, there seem to be two main approaches to dealing with stress:

1. DO SOMETHING. Be efficient, set priorities, use time wisely, etc.

2. DO NOTHING. Relax, escape, let go, let God.

Sometimes it really helps to *take action* to relieve your stress. I can recall years ago when my mother used to come from Michigan to California for visits and while she was here she would try to do things that she thought would help me.

One of her favorite tasks was rearranging all my cupboards. Because I am left-handed, my mother always decided everything was in the wrong place. So she would switch the kitchen all around to make it handy for right-handed people—like herself. When she got my kitchen organized, she asked if she could work in the yard. Unfortunately for Mom, the yard was in good shape, but Bill thought of a way to keep her busy because she was driving him a little bonkers, too.

Before Bill would leave for work early in the morning, he would be out there in the yard, shaking our two trees and causing the leaves to fall. I suppose the neighbors wondered what Bill was doing at 7:00 A.M., shaking the trees in our backyard. I'm not sure that we ever told them he was just trying to give his mother-in-law something to do—rake up the leaves—so she could feel "helpful" by making herself useful.

Mom never stopped trying to help. Ironically, when people try to help, they often cause more stress than if they hadn't bothered. In her case, this was, oh, so true. During one of her visits, Barney, who was quite young at the time, had a dreadful cold and cough. Mom offered to stay home with him while we went to church and I gave her some medicated, *non-rubbing* Musterole to put on his chest. Like most mothers, she felt she knew all about taking care of children, and she neglected to heed my advice and my clear instructions that this was the *non-rubbing* kind of Musterole.

She went ahead and massaged it right into Barney, rubbing around and around his face, ears, chest, and throat. When we got home from church, Barney's face was swollen, his eyes were puffy, his ears burned a bright red, and his chest was on fire. At least she hadn't put on an old-fashioned mustard plaster on him to "hold in the heat." Mom had good intentions—she just didn't always listen to instructions.

## Cat Food Salad and Stress

Another good way to cope with stress is to be flexible. When you think about it, a lot of stress is caused just because folks can't change their plans, can't take less than they had planned to, can't do less than they had planned to do, etc.

But sometimes, stress causes you to change your plans because you really don't have any choice.

Some years ago, we had a Swedish girl who came to live with us. Helga had relatives here, but they loaned her to us to help with the housework while she learned English. Helga stayed with us for almost a year and during that time we enjoyed taking her around California and showing her the sights. Helga was slowly learning to speak some English but hadn't mastered READING it yet.

One day I was planning on having about twenty gals over for a shower/luncheon to honor one girl who was getting married. While I went out shopping for decorations, I left Helga at home making up the tuna salad that would be the main dish for our luncheon. Helga loved to make special creations out of radishes by making them into rosebuds. She was also skilled at turning celery and carrots into fancy shapes. The plan was for Helga to make a bed of lettuce, radish rosebuds, carrot and celery curls, and then top it off with a big scoop of tuna fish mixed with hard-boiled eggs and garnished with olives.

As I came through the door with the decorations, I was overwhelmed by a terrible smell that seemed to permeate the entire house. I went into the kitchen and there on the counter were all of the luncheon salad plates, beautifully assembled, and ready to serve. But the fishy odor was overwhelming!

I picked up one of the salads, took a strong whiff, and then realized what had happened. Quickly, I opened the cupboard where we kept the trash, and there were at least a dozen empty cans that had once held CAT FOOD. I should have realized that Helga could easily mix up cat food with tuna fish. After all, the cat-food can had a picture of a little fish on it and it was natural enough for Helga, who couldn't read English, to think that she had the right can. Helga was so proud of how lovely her salad plates looked with the radish rosebuds and the carrot and celery curls, all sprouting around each scoop of cat food. She had worked hard to make everything special, but the fishy SMELL was enough to knock your socks off!! I was reminded of a sign I saw at a fish market: "Our fish are so fresh, it makes you wanna *smack 'em!*"

With twenty women due to arrive in just a few minutes, you might say, I was under STRESS. I decided the only thing to do was to take everyone out to lunch at a cafeteria while we left all the windows open to air out the house. We would come back later for the shower festivities, hoping that most of the smell would be gone.

It all worked out pretty well. We could still smell cat food as the guest of honor opened her shower gifts, but we all had a hearty laugh about the mixup. Without a doubt, it was a shower we'll all remember, and it reinforced for me the importance of being flexible under stress.

## Diabetes—Sword of Damocles

There are lots of ways to cope with stress. On the next page are twenty different tips for dealing with stress ACTIVELY by doing something, or taking care of something. On page 97 are twenty EASY-GOING ways to deal with stress by slowing down and taking time for things that are relaxing and restful.

---

TWENTY ACTIVE WAYS TO COPE WITH STRESS

Following are twenty ways to cope with stress that involve taking decisive action, doing something to deal with whatever may be causing stress in your life.

Get up fifteen minutes earlier . . . Prepare for the morning the night before . . . Set appointments ahead . . . Make duplicate keys . . . Always make copies of important papers . . . Repair anything that doesn't work properly . . . Ask for help with the jobs you dislike . . . Have goals for yourself . . . Stop a bad habit . . . Ask someone to be your "vent partner" . . . Do it today . . . Plant a tree . . . Feed the birds . . . Stand up and stretch . . . Memorize a joke . . . Exercise every day . . . Learn the words to a new song . . . Get to work early . . . Clean out one closet . . . Write a note to a faraway friend.[3]

---

As I cope with my latest "stress companion"—diabetes—I find myself trying to balance action by taking time to slow down. There is a lot of stress in just HAVING diabetes, a relatively unfamiliar disease to the general public because only about five million people are affected. When I was diagnosed with adult-onset diabetes a few years ago, I asked my doctor, "Is there any way to fix it?"

"No, you'll have it forever."

"You mean there's no cure?"

"No," said my doctor, "and in all probability it will get worse. Your pancreas is pooped out and isn't working any more. You'll have to change your whole lifestyle to adjust to this."

"Adjusting" to diabetes means continually balancing out your diet, doing proper exercise, and "avoiding stress." You have to poke a hole in your finger five or six times a day to monitor your blood sugar. You get up in the morning and your first thought is, *Time to prick my finger and check my blood sugar.*

---

TWENTY RELAXING WAYS TO DEAL WITH STRESS

Following are twenty ways to deal with stress that can help you relax and try to "go with the flow" rather than getting tense or upright.

Tickle a baby . . . Pet a friendly dog or cat . . . Don't know all the answers . . . Look for the silver lining . . . Say something nice to someone . . . Teach a kid to fly a kite . . . Walk in the rain . . . Schedule play time into every day . . . Take a bubble bath . . . Read a poem . . . Listen to a symphony . . . Play patty cake with a toddler . . . Take a different route to work . . . Remember that stress is an attitude . . . Remember you always have options . . . Have a support network of people, places, and things . . . Quit trying to "fix" other people . . . Get enough sleep . . . Talk less and listen more . . . Relax, take each day at a time, you have the rest of your life to live.[4]

---

You have to keep careful track of what you eat, and if you eat the wrong thing today, you'd better be sure you don't do it again tomorrow! You have to keep your blood sugar regulated all the time and hopefully you will avoid some of the severe complications of diabetes.

Diabetes is like the sword of Damocles dangling above your head. Blindness, amputations, kidney problems, or neuropathy (lack of feeling in the feet) are just a few of the possible problems it can cause.

This poem by Ernest Lowe vividly describes what it's like to have diabetes:

> To be told
> your cells are unhealthy,
> your capillaries . . . even your blood . . .
>     well, maybe not unhealthy,
> just abnormal.

To be told you will most likely
live a few years less
and maybe you shouldn't have a kid,
in fact—if you get a bad doc—
maybe you should be sterilized.

To be told you have to get under control
while people ask you
    "Why are you so controlling?"

To be told you can live just like normal
people if you will just watch your blood
sugar, food, salt consumption, exercise, urine,
schedule, feet, and stress,
            24 hours a day,
            7 days a week,
            365 days a year . . .
That's what it's like
to be told you're diabetic!

        Now then,
        what can I tell myself?
They're talking statistics
and I'm living life,
my life like no other.

        I tell myself
I make choices and sure I'm in
control, with every choice I make,
even the ones they call wrong.

        I tell myself
this so-called burden
is also a gift to remind me
    how precious each day can be—
    the gift of knowing I'll live till I die.

That's what it's like to remember
    I'm human.[5]

## Scripture Washes Away Life's Doo-Doo

Just knowing you have diabetes is stressful. You are always wondering, did I eat enough grams of THIS? Did I avoid enough grams of THAT?

I've often smiled over my doctor's advice to "avoid stress." Any emotional hassle, such as an accident or an argument, and your blood sugar shoots way up. For the diabetic, this can cause complications.

So I try to avoid controversial things and just concentrate on helping people. But there is no way to get away from the

stress of Spatula Ministries. The phone rings constantly, mail is always arriving, and new voices are pouring out their fresh heartbreaks. Fortunately, talking on the phone doesn't seem that stressful, maybe because the other person is doing most of the talking and crying while I am just listening.

Our monthly Spatula Ministries meetings do cause a lot of stress, however. When fifty to sixty people are sitting in one room letting out their anger, hurt, and anguish, it can get stressful, believe me! Then there are the "after-meeting" conversations that sometimes take hours. Sometimes folks ask how *I* get replenished. They want to know what I do to have my emotional tank filled.

One of my favorite ways to renew my spirit is to take a warm bubblebath with my tape player nearby so I can listen to my favorite Christian music or the reading of Scripture. The combination of water and music is therapy for me. I also have several videos featuring beautiful scenery with a narrator reading passages like Isaiah 26:3 (TLB): "He will keep in perfect peace all those who trust in Him, whose thoughts turn often to the Lord!"

My tapes and videos allow Scripture to come in and cleanse me after living in the daily doo-doo of life. We need to be renewed and refreshed, and I find that Scripture is like water washing over me. I feel as though I've had a spiritual bath that cleanses my mind and soul, and I'm reminded of a verse in Ezekiel where God says: "I will sprinkle clean water on you, and you will be clean; I will cleanse you from all your impurities. . . ."[6]

The other night I sat in a restaurant parking lot until 2:00 A.M. helping a young man dying of AIDS plan his funeral. It was too difficult for his parents, but he needed to talk about it. Although listening to him was stressful, I came home feeling honored because he wanted me to help make plans for what he knew was coming.

Afterward, I came home, and as I watched a Scripture video, I felt God's Word replenishing my joy.

When speaking for women's groups, I say, "You may think you have it all together, but then something will come along to remind you that you NEVER have it all together, no matter how old, no matter how much experience you have. The older you get, the more you realize that you get one wall up and the other wall falls down. If it's not a physical problem, it'll be emotional or mental. The point is that *you have to accept what life hands you.* You'll never have all the walls up at the same time— at least not on this earth anyway."

We live in a broken world. That's why Proverbs 3:5, 6 makes so much sense:

> TRUST IN THE LORD WITH ALL YOUR HEART,
> AND LEAN NOT ON YOUR OWN UNDERSTANDING;
> IN ALL YOUR WAYS ACKNOWLEDGE HIM,
> AND HE SHALL DIRECT YOUR PATHS. (NKJV)

The stress will always be there, but God will always be there, too, and that gives you the edge!

## Splish/Splash . . .

WORRY IS WASTING TODAY'S TIME
TO CLUTTER UP TOMORROW'S OPPORTUNITIES
WITH YESTERDAY'S TROUBLES.

\* \* \* \* \* \*

THERE WILL BE NO CRISIS NEXT WEEK.
MY SCHEDULE IS ALREADY FULL.

\* \* \* \* \* \*

THE PEOPLE WHO TELL YOU NEVER TO LET LITTLE THINGS WORRY YOU HAVE NEVER TRIED SLEEPING IN THE SAME ROOM WITH A MOSQUITO.

\* \* \* \* \* \*

IF YOU TREAT EVERY SITUATION
AS A LIFE-AND-DEATH MATTER,
YOU WILL DIE A LOT OF TIMES.

\*　\*　\*　\*　\*　\*

WE CRUCIFY OURSELVES BETWEEN TWO THIEVES:
REGRET FOR YESTERDAY
AND FEAR OF WHAT TOMORROW MAY BRING.

\*　\*　\*　\*　\*　\*

NOTHING IS IMPOSSIBLE
TO THE PEOPLE
WHO DON'T HAVE TO
DO IT THEMSELVES.

\*　\*　\*　\*　\*　\*

I'M NOT GOING TO WORRY
UNLESS THE ANIMALS START LINING UP
TWO BY TWO FOR THE NEXT SPACE SHUTTLE!

\*　\*　\*　\*　\*　\*

How often we look upon God as our last and feeblest re-
source. We go to Him because we have nowhere else to go. And
then we learn that the storms of life have driven us, not upon
the rocks, but into the desired haven.

George MacDonald

\*　\*　\*　\*　\*　\*

THINGS WILL PROBABLY COME OUT ALL RIGHT,
BUT SOMETIMES IT TAKES STRONG NERVES
JUST TO WATCH.

\*　\*　\*　\*　\*　\*

FAITH MAKES
THE UPLOOK GOOD,
THE OUTLOOK BRIGHT,
THE INLOOK FAVORABLE,
AND THE FUTURE GLORIOUS.

\* \* \* \* \* \*

Don't worry about anything; instead, pray about everything; tell God your needs and don't forget to thank him for his answers. (Phil. 4:6, TLB)

# Laugh and the World Laughs with You . . . Cry and You Simply Get Wet!

*Nothing beats fun.*

Dear Barbara,

I received your book as a Mother's Day gift. I haven't read a book in years, but this one is so good I couldn't put it down. I also haven't laughed in about seven years. I thought I forgot how.

\* \* \* \* \* \*

Dear Barbara and Gopher Bill,

I am single, never married, no children, but your answers to dealing with some of your problems were a real encouragement to me. I really enjoyed the humor in your book. Laughter really is a pick-me-up.

\* \* \* \* \* \*

Dear Spatula Ministries,

I've been living a shaky life . . . grief, pain . . . all jumbled up inside. I felt like I couldn't share because so much had happened . . . I felt like a Christian "freak." I found your book at the grocery store. I've laughed like I haven't for three years. I've also wept until the grief felt gone. Thank you for sharing and giving me a glimpse of hope.

\* \* \* \* \* \*

Dear Barbara,

I needed your words the day I read them for the laughter that parts of the book triggered. There truly is NOTHING like a deep, gut-stirring, tear-streaming laugh. I thank you!

\* \* \* \* \* \*

These letters are all reflections on what God said long ago: "A happy heart is like good medicine. But a broken spirit drains your strength" (Prov. 17:22, NCV). Recently I had the opportunity to share my story at a retreat, and afterward the gals filled out an evaluation of what they liked about the weekend. As I looked over a copy of my "report card," one phrase kept popping up: "I loved the humor and the chance to laugh." Everywhere I go there is the same response. Folks do love to laugh, and when you think about what laughter can do, it's easy to see why.

## A Good Laugh Is the Best Medicine

Someone said the best doctors in the world are Dr. Diet, Dr. Quiet, and Dr. Merryman. Laughter actually produces positive physiological results. For example, it exercises the lungs and stimulates the circulatory system. When you laugh, your body is revitalized by what could be called internal massage. Laughter, as somebody said, is like jogging on the inside.

Because laughter is therapeutic, hospitals are developing "laughter programs" and doctors are actually "prescribing" mirth as a way to get well. At Johns Hopkins Hospital, they show "Candid Camera," "The Three Stooges," and other comedy films on closed-circuit television. Down in Texas at one Catholic hospital, the nuns tell funny stories to patients on a daily basis to help them feel better.[1]

In his book, *Anatomy of an Illness as Perceived by the Patient: Reflections on Healing and Regeneration,* Norman Cousins told about his battle with an incurable and excruciatingly painful disease. His body's collagen, the fibrous material holding his cells together, was deteriorating, and he was, in his own words, "becoming unstuck." Gravel-like substances under his skin produced nodules on his body and he was having difficulty moving his neck, hands, arms, fingers, and legs. Doctors put the odds for his recovery at five hundred to one.

With his doctor's approval, Cousins decided to treat himself by eating healthy food, taking vitamins, particularly vitamin C, and undergoing what he called "laugh therapy." Because he wasn't sure the other patients in the hospital were ready for his new approach, he checked out of the hospital and into a hotel room, bringing along a lot of "Candid Camera" clips, Marx brothers movies, and cartoons—anything that might make him laugh. He watched all these again and again and after a while he developed a formula. If he laughed hard for ten minutes straight, he would have two hours of painlessness. Cousins amazed doctors by eventually recovering.[2]

## How Laughing Controls Pain

The experts say that laughter helps control pain in four ways: (1) by distracting attention, (2) by reducing tension, (3) by changing expectations, and (4) by increasing the production of endorphins, the body's natural pain killers.[3]

When you laugh, it takes your mind off the pain and actually creates a degree of anesthesia. You don't feel the pain as much because your attention is elsewhere.

All of us are familiar with how anxiety, worry, and stress can cause tension in the head and the neck muscles; the result is often another Excedrin headache. Laughter reduces muscle tension and has even been known to have the same effect on a headache as aspirin or other pain relievers.

Another thing about laughter is its ability to change your expectations, or, in other words, change your attitude. In a way, laughter is like a shock absorber that eases the blows of life.

Dr. David Bresler, director of the UCLA Pain Control Unit, says that pain is the most common, expensive, and disabling disorder in the United States, but that you can eliminate a great deal of pain by simply changing your mind. "Almost always, people who have chronic pain are also depressed," says Dr. Bresler. "It's not just their lower back that hurts, their life hurts and they have places that hurt in their lower back."[4]

In other words, our general attitude toward life is directly related to our sensitivity to pain. Laughter and humor are related to a positive outlook and a will to live.

Laughter could be called a tranquilizer with no side effects. When you laugh, the pituitary gland releases those endorphins mentioned earlier, which are "chemical cousins" of drugs like heroin and morphine.[5] The more you laugh, the more the level of endorphins in the brain increases and the more your perception of pain decreases. Laughter causes your body to literally produce its own anesthetic.

Not only is laughter healing, it helps keep you in shape and able to fight off disease. One Stanford professor discovered that laughter is like good exercise—equal to running, swimming, or rowing. Dr. William Fry's research showed that laughter increases the heart rate, improves circulation, and works the muscles of the face and stomach. Dr. Fry learned that if he spent ten seconds doing hard belly laughing, it would raise his heart rate to the same level he would reach in ten minutes of rowing (a very strenuous exercise). Thus, he estimates that if you laugh one hundred times a day, it will have the same training effect as a ten-minute workout on a rowing machine.[6]

## Laughter Is Good for Your Soul

Laughter is not only good for the body, it's good for the soul. Psychologically, the ability to see humor in a situation is as important as the laughter, itself. A sense of humor can help you overlook the unattractive, tolerate the unpleasant, cope with the unexpected, and smile through the unbearable. A genuine sense of humor is the pole that adds balance to our steps as we walk the tightrope of life. And, if we happen to fall into one of life's inevitable cesspools, a healthy sense of humor can help us cope. I like the saying:

> OUR FIVE SENSES ARE INCOMPLETE
> WITHOUT THE SIXTH—A SENSE OF HUMOR.

Having a sense of humor doesn't mean that you go around laughing at everything. A person with a sense of humor doesn't make jokes out of life; she only sees the ones that are already there. In other words, you can see the funny side along with the serious side.

My friend, Marilyn Meberg, who is a conference speaker as well as a family counselor, says that many of us take ourselves too seriously. We worry about always looking good, correct, and dignified. The result is that we miss out on a lot of fun.

Speaking at one weekend conference, Marilyn said, "There are things that will happen to you that cause you to feel you have lost control. But if you can laugh at yourself and the circumstances, you've regained control. Circumstances will not control you if you turn them around and make something funny out of them. My suggestion to you is that there are many, many times in your daily experience when you can turn your situation around and laugh. Laugh at the situation. Laugh at yourself. When you do, you're in charge instead of it being in charge of you."[7]

That reminds me of something else that's well worth remembering:

HAPPY IS THE WOMAN WHO CAN LAUGH AT HERSELF;
SHE WILL NEVER CEASE TO BE AMUSED.

I believe that if we can divide our problems into those that can be solved quickly and those that cannot, we will have come a long way toward relaxing when confronted with things that we cannot change. Humor is God's weapon against worry, anxiety, and fear. Remember that:

FEAR IS THE DARKROOM
WHERE NEGATIVES ARE DEVELOPED.

Job said with subtle wisdom, "For the thing I greatly feared has come upon me, and what I dreaded has happened. . . ."[8] Negative thoughts give birth to negative ordeals, and positive thoughts yield positive experiences. Laughing people can survive and land on their feet. Those who cannot laugh will stay in the cesspool of despair.

As somebody said, your day goes the way the corners of your mouth turn. Life is like a mirror. If we frown at it, it frowns back. If we smile, it returns the greeting. Every Christmas I like to remember that the best Yuletide decoration is being wreathed in smiles.

Laughter helps us love one another. In his best-selling book, *Loving Each Other*, Leo Buscaglia said: "A bond of love is easy to find in an environment of joy. When we laugh together, we bypass reason and logic as the clown does. We speak a universal language. We feel closer to one another."[9]

Glad and happy sharing creates *koinonia*—a Greek word that means "loving fellowship." By contrast, sad, depressing conversations are counterproductive. Who of us has not watched tensions dissolve in the presence of love and humor? We see this happen continually in our Spatula meetings. Deep pain is present. Abscesses are festering with anguish and pain, waiting to be opened and drained. Sometimes the depressing stories can become almost overwhelming, but then somebody will say something humorous and it will pick up the mood of everyone there. We all feel lifted above the pain we are bearing together.

For example, at a recent meeting of our Spatula chapter, a grief-stricken father was sharing about his son, who had decided to become a girl. He was going to be taking his son to dinner and his son had already let him know that he would be coming "in drag," that is, dressed as a woman.

Heartbroken, with tears in his eyes, the father said, "I don't know what to do. How can I handle this?"

There were about fifty people in the room, but you could hear a pin drop. Finally, the silence became so unbearable I decided somebody had to say something; so, to lighten up the situation, I suggested, "Maybe you could wear your wife's clothes and your son would feel more comfortable."

There was a moment of stunned silence. Then somebody started to laugh, and pretty soon we were all laughing, including the father. Humor had stepped in to save the situation when logic or good, practical advice wouldn't have helped a great deal. Besides, there is no "good, practical advice" in such an impossible situation.

There are many reasons to laugh, so go ahead. Since it takes forty-three muscles to frown but only seventeen muscles to smile, why not conserve energy? Keep this in mind:

> AN OPTIMIST LAUGHS TO FORGET;
> THE PESSIMIST FORGETS TO LAUGH.

Here's another thought that may help you keep things in perspective:

> There are two days in every week about which we should not worry, two days which should be kept free from fear and apprehension.
>
> One of the two days is YESTERDAY, with its mistakes and cares, its faults and blunders, its aches and pains. Yesterday has passed forever beyond our control. All the money in the world cannot bring back yesterday. We cannot undo a single act we performed. We cannot erase a single word we said. Yesterday is gone.

The other day we should not worry about is TOMORROW, with its possible adversities, its burden, its large promise and poor performance. Tomorrow is also beyond our immediate control. Tomorrow's sun will rise, either in splendor or behind a mask of clouds—but it *will* rise. Until it does, we have no stake in tomorrow, for it is yet unborn.

This leaves only one day—TODAY—anyone can fight the battles of just one day. It is only when you and I add the burdens of those two awful eternities—yesterday and tomorrow—that we break down.

It is not the experience of today that drives us mad—it is remorse or bitterness for something which happened yesterday and the dread of what tomorrow may bring.

Let us, therefore, live but one day at a time.

Source unknown

MOTORCYCLE
COWASOCKY

Just a reminder that we are all udderly flawed !

And, I might add, let's live it with smiles on our faces!

It's funny what becomes funny to us. When you think about it, we really laugh about serious things: money, family, parents, children, sex—even death. (Perhaps you have heard of the funeral director who signed all his letters, "Eventually yours.") Life is full of tensions, stress, and grim realities. When we need a break now and then, how do we spell relief?

L-A-U-G-H

As somebody said, laughter is the cheapest luxury we have. It clears up the blood, expands the chest, electrifies the nerves, clears away the cobwebs from the brain, and gives the whole system a good cleansing. I really believe laughter is the sweetest music that ever greeted the human ear, and I also believe God loves to hear our laughter.

## Out of the Mouths of Babes

I'm continually receiving stories, jokes, clippings, and quips, and one of the most popular categories is children. Kids cause their share of pain and worry, but they're also good for laughs (fortunately for them!).

I ran across a story (I don't know who wrote it) about some children who started dropping coins into a wishing well, whispering aloud their wishes.

"I wish I had a puppy," said one.

"I wish I had a race car," said another.

A boy about ten years of age walked up and looked thoughtfully into the well. Then, grudgingly, he tossed in his coin and muttered, "I wish I had a magnet."

President Lyndon Johnson used to tell a story about a little boy who wanted some money very badly because his daddy had died and his mother was having a hard time making ends meet. The boy wrote a letter to God, asking for a hundred dollars to help his mama. He mailed the letter and it wound up on the Postmaster General's desk. The gentleman was so touched he slipped a twenty-dollar bill into an envelope and mailed it back to the youngster. Two weeks later, another letter to God from the little boy wound up on the Postmaster General's desk. It said, "Much obliged for all you've done, but the next time, please don't route it through Washington because they deducted eighty dollars."[10]

Another one of my favorites comes from a mother who has four grown children. One is living with a girl and they aren't married, another is an alcoholic, a third is on drugs, and the youngest is gay. She told me, "Barb, I should never have had kids. I should have had RABBITS. At least THAT way I would have gotten one good meal out of the deal."

## Goofs Are Always Good for a Laugh

It's fun to collect funny sayings and improper uses of words, sometimes called malapropisms. One list I found included these samples:

- If you can't do it right, do it yourself.
- Arrogance is bliss.
- Abstinence makes the heart grow fonder.
- No news travels fast.
- Every clown has a silver lining.
- Run it up the flag pole and see who sits on it.
- Am I my brother's beeper?
- No man can serve two masters with one stone.
- Rome wasn't burned in a day.
- It's on the fork of my tongue.
- Take it with a grain of truth.
- That's the frosting on the gravy.
- People who live in glass houses shouldn't throw sour grapes.[11]

But one of my all-time favorites about goofs is an old story that has made the rounds, especially among newspaper publishers and editors who have to live with an irritating fact of life called the typographical error. We've all seen typos in newspapers, but here is an example of how an error got into the classified section of a small-town daily, and the more they tried to correct it, the more disastrous it became:

(Monday) FOR SALE—R. D. Jones has one sewing machine for sale. Phone 555–0707 after 7 P.M. and ask for Mrs. Kelly who lives with him cheap.

(Tuesday) NOTICE—We regret having erred in R. D. Jones's ad yesterday. It should have read: One sewing machine for sale. Cheap: 555–0707 and ask for Mrs. Kelly who lives with him after 7 P.M.

(Wednesday) NOTICE—R.D. Jones has informed us that he has received several annoying telephone calls because of the error we made in his classified ad yesterday. His ad stands corrected as follows: FOR SALE—R. D. Jones has one sewing machine for sale. Cheap. Phone 555–0707 and ask for Mrs. Kelly who loves with him.

(Thursday) NOTICE—I, R. D. Jones, have NO sewing machine for sale. I SMASHED IT. Don't call 555–0707, as the telephone has been disconnected. I have NOT been carrying on with Mrs. Kelly. Until yesterday she was my housekeeper, but she quit.[12]

## Laughs from the Book of Parables

The Bible may be the world's best seller, but it isn't necessarily always the world's best-studied book. People get biblical knowledge mixed up, as this story shows:

A freshman entering Bible college was asked what part of the Bible he liked best.

"Well, I like the New Testament best," he answered.

"What book do you like in the New Testament?" the interviewer wanted to know.

"Oh, by far, I like the Book of Parables best," the freshman replied.

"Would you kindly relate one of those parables to me?" the interviewer asked.

The freshman complied, saying, "Once upon a time, a man went down from Jerusalem to Jericho and fell among thieves. And the thorns grew up and choked that man. And he went on and met the Queen of Sheba and she gave that man a thousand talents of gold and silver and a hundred changes of raiment. And he got in his chariot and drove furiously, and as he was driving under a big tree his hair got caught in a limb and left him hanging there.

"And he hung there many days and many nights and the ravens brought him food to eat and water to drink. And one night while he was hanging there asleep, his wife, Delilah, came along and cut off his hair. And he dropped and fell on stony ground. And it began to rain, and it rained forty days and forty nights. And he hid himself in a cave. And he went out and met a man and said, 'Come and take supper with me in my cave.' But the man answered, 'I cannot for I have married a wife.' And the cave-dweller went out into the highways and byways and compelled people to come in.

"And he went on and came to Jericho and he saw Queen Jezebel sitting high up in a window and when she saw him she laughed. And he said, 'Throw her down.' He said, 'Throw her down' again. And they threw her down seventy times seven. And of the fragments they picked up twelve baskets. And now, what I want to know is, Whose wife will she be on the day of resurrection?"

Source unknown

The hapless freshman's biblical confusion might make us smile; and it might remind some of us of how we've gotten certain biblical concepts a little twisted around ourselves. But on occasion I like to balance this kind of church humor with something I found while traveling in Nevada not too long ago.

High on a hill above Reno stands a large church called the Reno Christian Fellowship. Like a beacon, it overlooks all the gaudy, brilliantly flashing casino signs in the streets below. From this pinnacle, you can view the entire city and then see the twinkling lights fade off into the desert beyond.

My daughter-in-love, Shannon, had been to this church, and when I told her I was speaking there, she told me to be sure to see the sign posted as you start down the driveway to leave the church.

When I finished speaking and we were preparing to leave the parking lot, I suddenly remembered and said to Bill, "We must be sure to look for the sign Shannon told us about." As we started down the driveway that would take us to the road leading into Reno, there it was in large letters:

YOU ARE NOW ENTERING THE MISSION FIELD!

Reading that sign gave me goose bumps because its meaning reaches far beyond the Reno city limits. WHEREVER we live—THAT is our mission field!

## When Life Gets Out of Control—Laugh

Marilyn Meberg tells a story that beautifully illustrates how we may be facing circumstances that seem to be controlling us. It describes how we can regain control by finding something to giggle about that gives us strength to get through the moment. It's not that we try to giggle away grief or death, but it is true that we can sometimes alleviate a measure of pain by finding something to laugh at for the moment.

Marilyn's mother died recently and prior to her death she requested that her body be cremated rather than having the usual funeral with people gazing upon her corpse and saying things like, "Oh, doesn't she look NATURAL!"

Marilyn did exactly as her mother asked and her body was cremated. Later, the mortuary called and asked Marilyn to come in and claim her mother's ashes. She and her husband, Ken, drove down to the mortuary and, while he waited in the car, she went inside. A man handed her a container about the size of a shoe box telling her, "Here are the cremains."

The box had her mother's name on it, the date of her birth, and the day she died. Carrying it gave Marilyn an eerie feeling.

Everything she had known of her mother in her earthly state was now supposedly shifting around in this little box.

She went out the door of the mortuary and walked toward the car, where she could see Ken looking at her from the front seat. Marilyn's husband had always adored her mother and she could tell he felt awkward about what she was carrying. So did Marilyn. And she had other feelings, too—pain, hurt, grief. The whole thing was becoming too grim and too hard to deal with.

Marilyn opened the car door, saw the look on Ken's face, and simultaneously assessed her own feelings. She felt a strong need to "lighten the moment," so she decided to put the cremains box on the backseat. As she did so, she leaned over warmly and said, "Mom, do you need a seatbelt?"

"MARILYN!" was all her husband could say, but Marilyn didn't mind. She had been hearing him say that for years whenever she did anything a little off the wall, which was pretty often.

Nonetheless, her concern about a seatbelt for Mom did the trick for the moment and lifted their spirits just a bit. She recalls, "It wasn't that I was being irreverent about my mother, or her cremains. It was just for those few seconds I needed to lighten the moment and feel that I had a measure of control rather than having the circumstances control me."[13]

Humor can lighten the grim, painful, and frustrating moments of life, as well as the times when no hope is in sight. The apostle Paul faced plenty of moments that were grim, painful, frustrating, and even hopeless. Yet he wrote: "We rejoice in the hope of the glory of God" (Rom. 5:2, NIV).

I believe laughter is like a needle and thread. Deftly used, it can patch up just about everything. That's why I urge folks to keep a joy box for mementos, greeting cards, clippings, and little knickknacks of every imaginable description, all of which can bring a smile or even a chuckle, especially when you're feeling discouraged. Years ago my joy box grew into a JOY ROOM that now takes up half of the mobile home where we live. Whenever I enter my Joy Room, I not only find smiles, I find hope.

On the back of the main door to the Joy Room is a huge sign with my favorite motto: "WHATEVER, LORD!" Beneath the sign sits a doll that looks like a little old lady, and she asks, "Dear God, if I give all my love away, can I have a refill?"

On a shelf nearby sits a darling little alarm clock/music box that can be set to wake you up to such tunes as, "It's a Small, Small World"; "Heigh Ho, Heigh Ho, It's Off to Work We Go"; "Zippity Do Dah"; and "Super-Cali-Fragil-Istic-Expi-Ali-Docious." Wouldn't every mom love to have one of these little clocks to help get her kids up for school?

A few feet away sits a little monkey on a perch, and when you turn the handle, his tail goes up and down and he makes funny noises. His sign says: "WELCOME TO THE NUT HOUSE."

A lot of friends send me sayings and mottoes done in cross-stitch. One of my favorites has two darling little bears surrounding the phrase, "Love Makes Life More Bearable."

Since *So, Stick a Geranium In Your Hat and Be Happy* came out, almost every time I speak at a banquet, I seem to pick up another geranium hat. I now have twenty-one of them on display in my Joy Room, reminding me of friends across the country.

My Joy Room walls are filled with many other signs, mottoes, and plaques. A few of my favorites include:

LIFE IS TOO IMPORTANT TO BE TAKEN SERIOUSLY.

\* \* \* \* \* \*

I am wonderful, marvelous, extra-special, unique, first-rate, exceptional, outrageous, surprising, superlative—and, above all—HUMBLE.

\* \* \* \* \* \*

MID-LIFE CRISIS:
WHEN MORTGAGE PAYMENTS AND THE TUITION BILL
EQUAL MORE THAN YOU MAKE.

*   *   *   *   *   *

THINGS ARE LOOKING UP . . .
I'M NOW ONLY TWO WEEKS BEHIND.

*   *   *   *   *   *

Another plaque that I especially like is a Scripture verse carved in wood by Bob Davies, my good friend at Love in Action:

> In the fear of the Lord, one has strong confidence, and His children will have a refuge.
>
> Proverbs 14:26, RSV

I also love the miniature wagon that sits in one corner with a sign painted on its side: "Lord, I need a push!" Another favorite is a hot-water bottle shaped like a woolly lamb. When filled he becomes fat and fluffy.

Almost everything in my Joy Room has been sent to me by someone. One special note mounted on the wall comes from a group of people in the Midwest who are all parents of homosexual children. They call themselves "The Humpty-Dumpties," and they sent me a poem that expresses perfectly the spirit of my Joy Room because it offers a smile along with a reminder of the hope we have through faith in God:

GOOD MORNING, HUMPTY DUMPTY, SIR,
HOW AMAZING, YOU'RE STILL HERE!
BY LEGEND YOU WERE SHATTERED,
HOW COHESIVE YOU APPEAR.

HUMPTY JUMPED, AND SAID WITH A SMILE,
"THE TALE OF HORSES AND MEN

WASN'T THE END! THE KING HIMSELF,
PUT ME TOGETHER AGAIN!"

## Keep Working On It

I opened this chapter with some comments from people who wrote to tell me how much they appreciate humor. Here is one more letter from a gal who really understands why nothing beats fun:

You don't know me from Adam, but I feel I know you as a dear friend who helped me through an incredible crisis.

Three weeks ago I had a mammogram. One day later I had a lumpectomy. Two weeks ago I had a mastectomy. Forty-eight hours later I was told the cancer had spread to the nodes. On that particular night (I was still in the hospital), I took a sleeping pill. Didn't work. I picked up the book my youngest daughter had brought in for me at the hospital. Your book. I read it through the night. I cried with you and laughed (especially at the pantyhose) with you. Whenever I feel I'm going into a downer I pick up your book again.

Following your advice I've tried to come up with (something) funny each day. Yesterday's was:

"I'll only go bra shopping if they'll give me 50 percent off."

Pretty corny, really, but I'm working on it.

A lot of funny things ARE corny, but keep working on it, because laughter can always be heard further than weeping. Always—and I mean always—TAKE TIME TO LAUGH. It is the music of the soul!

## Splish/Splash . . .

THERE IS HOPE FOR ANYONE WHO CAN LOOK IN A MIRROR
AND LAUGH AT WHAT HE SEES.

\*     \*     \*     \*     \*     \*

ONE THING YOU CAN SAY FOR KIDS, AT LEAST THEY DON'T BORE YOU WITH CUTE THINGS THEIR PARENTS SAID.[14]

\* \* \* \* \* \*

Phyllis Diller says life is tough: "Did you ever look in a mirror and wonder how your pantyhose got so wrinkled . . . and then remember you weren't wearing any?"[15]

\* \* \* \* \* \*

HUMOR IS THE HOLE
THAT LETS THE SAWDUST
OUT OF A STUFFED SHIRT.

\* \* \* \* \* \*

Do you know how you can tell if you are co-dependent? When you are dying, you see someone else's life pass before your eyes!

\* \* \* \* \* \*

The trouble with owning your own home is that, no matter where you sit, it seems you're looking at something you should be doing.[16]

\* \* \* \* \* \*

LITTLE BOY'S PRAYER

Dear God, take care of my family, take care of the whole world. And please, God, take care of Yourself, or we're all sunk.

\* \* \* \* \* \*

### A Confused Mother Writing to Her Son . . .

Dear Son,

Just a few lines to let you know that I'm still alive. I'm writing this letter slowly because I know you cannot read fast. You won't know the house when you come home—we've moved.

About your father—he has a lovely new job. He has five hundred men under him. He is cutting the grass at the cemetery.

There was a washing machine in the new house when we moved in, but it isn't working very good. Last week I put fourteen shirts into it, pulled the chain, and I haven't seen the shirts since.

Your sister, Mary, had a baby this morning. I haven't found out whether it's a boy or a girl, so I don't know whether you're a aunt or an uncle.

Your Uncle Dick drowned last week in a vat of whiskey in the Dublin Brewery. Some of his workmates dived in to save him, but he fought them off bravely. We cremated his body and it took three days to put out the fire.

Your father didn't have much to drink at Christmas. I put a bottle of castor oil in his pint of beer—it kept him going 'til New Year's Day.

I went to the doctor on Thursday and your father came with me. The doctor put a small tube into my mouth and told me to keep it shut for ten minutes. Your father offered to buy it from him.

It only rained twice last week. First for three days, and then for four days. Monday it was so windy that one of our chickens laid the same egg four times.

We had a letter yesterday from the undertaker. He said if the last installment wasn't paid on your grandmother within five days, up she comes.

Much love,
Mother

P.S. I was going to send you ten dollars, but I had already sealed the envelope.

\*     \*     \*     \*     \*     \*

HE WHO LAUGHS LAST
PROBABLY INTENDED TO TELL THE STORY HIMSELF.

\*    \*    \*    \*    \*    \*

. . . the cheerful heart has a continual feast. (Prov. 15:15, NIV)

## How Can I Be Over the Hill When I Never Even Got to the Top?

*You're young only once*
*but you can be immature forever[1]*

Wherever I go, women agree that two of their least favorite subjects are AGING and DIETING. My advice is to not let either one steal your joy. I decided a long time ago to stop fretting over increasing years and extra pounds and relish each day instead.

That doesn't mean I ignore healthy eating, nor does it mean that I seldom exercise. Before having diabetes made exercise a must for me, I was not a real enthusiast about working out. My idea of exercise was a good, brisk sit, or maybe wrestling with the cellophane wrapper on a Twinkie.

To paraphrase the bumper "snicker," every time I thought about exercise, I would lie down until the thought went away. Or Bill and I would ride our bikes—right down to the corner doughnut shop in the morning for coffee and maple bars.

In *So, Stick A Geranium in Your Hat and Be Happy*, I told about Bill buying me a fabulous Schwinn indoor bicycle and setting it up in our Joy Room, where I am well equipped to utilize my time and never feel bored as I ride my new bike. If I want to read, there is a book stand mounted on the handle bars. If I want to talk on the phone, my Kermit the Frog telephone is within easy reach. If I want to watch a certain TV program, a small television set is on a table nearby. If I don't want to do any of those things, I just might want to enjoy all the fun stuff that is in my Joy Room as I pedal away. My exercise bike is a cool, clean, and classy way to do what I'm supposed to be doing—being active and exercising.

While I sometimes do all the things mentioned above, my favorite pastime is putting some zing into my prayer life. I have a big map of the United States posted on a wall in front of my bike, and as I ride I make imaginary trips from one town to another, visiting Spatula friends who have written me. Every time I reach a town from which I have received a letter, I pray for the letter writers, asking God to be a help and comfort to them that day.

Lately, my daughter-in-love, Shannon, has drawn me a NEW map of the United States, which I call my "Joy Map." The distinctive feature about this map is that it has actual towns whose names suggest joy, laughter, or something pleasant. I have this map mounted on the wall next to the other one, and now, from time to time, I travel from Bliss to Ecstasy, from Utopia to Sublime, from Yum Yum to Comfort, or from Bountiful to Prosperity. As I visit towns like this in my imagination, it is no trick at all to cover long distances in a single ride. It's really fun to start at Happy, Texas, and wind up in Joyful, Mississippi!

## The Beach Ball Keeps Bobbing Back Up

Keeping weight down is a constant struggle for so many of us. Fighting the battle of the bulges is like holding a beach ball under water all your life. If you relax for just one minute, POW! Up it goes. Then it's a big struggle to get that ball back under the water again.

It seems that most of the time you're being forced to eat like a rabbit. After all, when you take all the fat, sugar, salt, and starch out of life, what's left except stuff that's high in tasteless fiber?

So, I have a lot of empathy for folks who struggle with weight and dieting. I know what it's like to struggle with wanting to eat and not being able to. The other day I ran across an old recording by the late Victor Buono, which included the following prayer by the tortured dieter:

> Lord, my soul is ripped with riot,
> Incited by my wicked diet.
> "We are what we eat," said a wise old man.
> Lord, if that's true, I'm a garbage can.
> I want to rise on Judgment Day, that's plain,
> But at my present weight I'll need a crane.
> So grant me strength that I may not fall
> Into the clutches of cholesterol.
> May my flesh with carrot curls be sated,
> That my soul may be polyunsaturated.
> And show me the light that I may bear witness
> To the President's Council on Physical Fitness.
> And oleo margarine I'll never mutter
> For the road to hell is spread with butter.
> And cream is cursed, and cake is awful,
> And Satan is hiding in every waffle.
> Mephistopheles lurks in provolone,
> The devil is in each slice of bologna.
> Beelzebub is a chocolate drop
> And Lucifer is a lollypop.
> Give me this day, my daily slice
> But cut it thin and toast it twice.
> I beg upon my dimpled knees,
> Deliver me from Ju Jubees
> And when my days of trial are done
> And my war with malted milks is won
> Let me stand with the saints in heaven
> In a shining robe, size thirty-seven!
> I can do it, Lord, if You'll show to me

The virtues of lettuce and celery
If You'll teach me the evil of mayonnaise
The sinfulness of hollandaise
And pasta Milanese
And potatoes à la Lyonnaise,
And crisp fried chicken from the South.
Lord, if You love me, SHUT MY MOUTH![2]

## Calories That DON'T Count

When you're dieting, there is nothing easier than rationalizing why it might be okay to eat "just one" and then a few more, even though you know the stuff is loaded with grams of fat and tons of calories. In my own collection of dieter's rationalizations is the following list of "calories that don't count."

1. **Food on Foot.** All food eaten while standing has no calories. Exactly why is not clear, but the current theory relates to gravity. The calories apparently bypass the stomach flowing directly down the legs, and through the soles of the feet into the floor, like electricity. Walking appears to accelerate this process, so that an ice cream bar or hot dog eaten at the state fair actually has a calorie deficit.

2. **TV Food.** Anything eaten in front of the TV has no calories. This may have something to do with radiation leakage, which negates not only the calories in the food but all recollections of having eaten it.

3. **Uneven Edges.** Pies and cakes should be cut neatly, in even wedges or slices. If not, the responsibility falls on the person putting them away to "straighten up the edges" by slicing away the offending irregularities, which have no calories when eaten.

4. **Balanced Food.** If you drink a diet soda with a candy bar, they cancel each other out.

5. **Left-Handed Food.** If you have a glass of punch in your right hand, anything eaten with the other hand has no calories. Several principles are at work here. First of all, you're probably standing up at a wedding reception (see Food on Foot). Then

there's the electronic field: A wet glass in one hand forms a negative charge to reverse the polarity of the calories attracted to
the other hand. It's not quite known how it works, but it's re-
versible if you're left-handed.

**6. Food for Medicinal Purposes.** Food used for medicinal
purposes NEVER counts. This includes hot chocolate, malted
milk, toast, and Sara Lee cheesecake.

**7. Whipped Cream, Sour Cream, Butter.** These all act as a
poultice that actually "draws out" the calories when placed on
any food, leaving them calorie-free. Afterward, you can eat the
poultice, too, as all calories are neutralized by it.

**8. Food on Toothpicks.** Sausage, mini-franks, cheese, and
crackers are all fattening UNLESS impaled on frilled toothpicks.
The insertion of a sharp object allows the calories to leak out
the bottom.

**9. Children's Food.** Anything produced, purchased, or intended for minors is calorie-free when eaten by adults. This cat-
egory covers a wide range, beginning with a spoonful of
baby-food custard, consumed for demonstration purposes, up
to and including cookies baked to send to college.

**10. Charitable Foods.** Girl Scout cookies, bake-sale cakes, ice-
cream socials, and church strawberry festivals all have a reli-
gious dispensation from calories.

**11. Custom-Made Food.** Anything somebody makes "just
for you" must be eaten regardless of the calories, because to do
otherwise would be uncaring and insensitive. Your kind intentions will not go unrewarded.[3]

## Dieting May Be Bad for Your Health

Like thousands of others, I've lost weight but always seem
to find it again. Medical experts call it the "yo-yo syndrome"
and I've had my share of those ups and downs. I keep dream-
ing of my slim, girlish figure, which is now carefully hidden
under a lot of padding. That's why my all-time favorite cartoon is the one on the following page.

A lot of "fluffy" folks must have been encouraged when *Time*
magazine came out with an article saying that much of the di-

eting that's been going on in recent years can be downright unhealthy. It said going through cycles of losing weight and then gaining it back can actually shorten your life. The famous Framingham Heart Study revealed that yo-yo dieters have a 70 percent higher risk of dying from heart disease than folks who are overweight but stay at a fairly steady level. The researchers concluded that the stress involved in losing and gaining weight back may increase your blood pressure and cholesterol levels, and that's why there is more danger of heart disease.[4]

The *Time* article didn't say that everyone should stop dieting, period. But what a lot of people need to do is set more realistic goals and not try to be the slim, sylph-like figures that are continually displayed on television. In 1990 the federal government came out with new tables listing healthy weights for men and women that allow for a range of thirty pounds or more at each height, and up to a sixteen-pound gain after you reach age thirty-five. Another statistic, released by the Calorie Control Council, says that the number of dieters in the United States has dropped from 65 million in 1986 to 48 million in 1991.[5]

My friend, Lynda, read about a fabulous idea for weight control. Doctors give you a balloon to swallow and then it is inflated in your stomach. Because the balloon keeps your stomach feeling "full," you don't want to eat and, of course, you lose weight. However, there is one STRING attached— literally! It is tied to the balloon and then extends back up the esophagus and hangs out the nose! (It seems the string is important in case the balloon breaks or there is some other emergency.)

Lynda and I began brainstorming on what we would do if we swallowed one of these balloons and had the string hanging out of our nose. What if one of our grandchildren decided to pull on it? Or what if it got caught in our toothbrushes?

Then we got a brilliant idea. Why not tie a brightly colored bead on the end of the string and let it dangle there, making a fashion statement? When you became tired of that, you could try stuffing the string up your nose out of sight, but then it would undoubtedly itch and eventually you'd sneeze and out the string would pop! If you were having trouble getting conversation started at some get-together that bead would surely do the trick!

The balloon idea sounded glorious except for that stupid string. Too bad. Lynda and I finally decided it was another miracle cure down the tube, or maybe you'd have to say up the nose. Whatever, we decided to skip on swallowing a balloon and keep on wrestling with the beach ball as best we can.

## All We Need Is Maturity

One reason we like to laugh at our struggles with weight is because it's better than crying. After all, if we were "disciplined and mature," we could fight off these childish desires to eat too much of what isn't very good for us. I'm all for being mature, but the trouble is, the word suggests sainthood.

If you're mature, you're patient and willing to forego instant gratification, even when it is a carton labeled "Håagen Dazs."

If you are mature, you can persevere, no matter how tough things get or how discouraged you might be.

If you're mature, you can handle frustration, discomfort, failure, and all other kinds of unpleasantness.

Humble people are mature. They are able to say, "I was wrong," and when they're right they don't have to say, "I told you so."

When you're mature, you can make decisions and then even follow through on them. And, of course, being mature means being dependable, keeping your word, and not bailing out with alibis.[6]

Maturity means growing up—and growing up is always optional. On the other hand, growing old is *not* optional—it's mandatory. It just happens whether you're ready for it or not. As Ashleigh Brilliant says:

> NOTHING IS MORE QUIET
> THAN THE SOUND OF HAIR GOING GREY.[7]

## Been to a Reunion Lately?

Because readers of the *Love Line* know I like to collect funny sayings and poems about aging, they are constantly telephoning or sending clippings in the mail. Today a lady called me and said she had just seen the following sign on a crematorium in, of all places, Palm Springs, California:

WE'RE HOT FOR YOUR BODY.

I've put together this commentary on aging, compiled from several sources:

> The material in dresses is so skimpy now, especially around the hips and waist, that it is almost impossible to reach one's shoelaces. And the sizes don't run the way they used to. The 12s and 14s are so much smaller.
>
> Even people are changing. They are so much younger than they used to be when I was their age. On the other hand, people my own age are so much older than I am.
>
> I ran into an old classmate the other day, and she has aged so much that she didn't recognize me.
>
> I got to thinking about the poor dear while I was combing my hair this morning, and in so doing I glanced at my own reflection. Really now, they don't even make good mirrors like they used to.

Another way to be reminded of the passing years is to go to a class reunion. You undoubtedly have been to one of these traumatic events, which are gatherings where you come to the conclusion that most of the people your own age are a lot older than you are. Another definition of a reunion is an event, "where everyone gets together to see who is falling apart."

I've never been to any kind of reunion—high school or college—but the other day I had the next best thing. While speaking at a conference I ran into two gentlemen who were in school with me over forty years ago. They were kind enough to say they recognized ME, but I must admit I could barely recognized THEM. It reminded me of how men are supposed to have three basic hair styles: parted, unparted, and departed. When I saw their bald pates, I was also reminded of the reason why men don't have to have facelifts: If they wait long enough, their face will grow right up through their hair!

Class reunions are times when nothing helps you recognize your old classmates as much as their nametags. It's such fun to come across pictures of myself when I was a young girl.

Somehow that sweet, young, high-school face seems more familiar to me than how I look now. I can still remember being so thin that I had to drink Ovaltine to gain weight. All I can say is, it sure did work!

## For All Those Born "Before"

A sure sign that you're getting up there is that you can remember back when things were different—a LOT different! I often share the following list with audiences at retreats and other programs. It's something I've put together from several sources—and it often grows as soon as I've shared it because someone will suggest another difference I can add:

### WHAT A DIFFERENCE FIFTY YEARS MAKES!

We were before the pill and the population explosion. We were before TV, penicillin, polio shots, antibiotics, and frisbees, before frozen food, nylon, dacron, Xerox, or Kinsey. We were before radar, fluorescent lights, credit cards, and ballpoint pens. For us, time-sharing meant togetherness, not computers or condominiums; a chip meant a piece of wood; hardware meant hardware; and software—well, software wasn't even a word.

In our time, closets were for clothes, not for coming out of, and being gay meant you were happy and carefree. In those days bunnies were small rabbits and rabbits were not Volkswagens.

We were before Batman, Rudolph the Red-Nosed Reindeer, and Snoopy. Before DDT and vitamin pills, disposable diapers, Jeeps, and the Jefferson nickel. We preceded Scotch tape, the Grand Coulee Dam, M&Ms, automatic transmissions, and Lincoln Continentals.

When we were in school, pizzas, Cheerios, frozen orange juice, instant coffee, and McDonald's were unheard-of. We thought fast food was what you ate during Lent.

We were before FM radio, tape recorders, electric typewriters, word processors, electronic music, digital clocks, and disco dancing.

We were before pantyhose and drip-dry clothes, before ice makers and dishwashers, clothes dryers, freezers, and electric blankets, before Hawaii and Alaska became states.

We were before Leonard Bernstein, yogurt, Ann Landers, plastics, hair spray, the forty-hour week, the minimum wage. We got married first and then lived together afterward. How quaint can you be?

In our day, grass was mowed, Coke was something you drank, and pot was something you cooked in.

We were before coin-operated vending machines, jet planes, helicopters, and interstate highways. In 1935 "made in Japan" meant junk, and the term "making out" referred to how you did on an exam.

We had fountain pens with bottles of real ink. We had stockings made of real silk with seams up the back that were never straight. We had saddle shoes and cars with rumble seats. We had corner ice-cream parlors with little tables and wire-back chairs where we had a choice of three flavors.

I have become unstuck in time, and in the springtime of my senility, I am a misfit. I don't like to jog. I don't know how to pump my own gas. My legs are white and my stockings are brown when the opposite is the style. I'm not into veggies or yoga or punk. My idea of a good time is to walk with a man, not jog with a Walkman.

I seek silence in a day when silence is as rare as a Gutenberg Bible. The man I live with is my husband and, after forty-two years, he's still the same one. How embarrassing!

## Grandma Ain't What She Used to Be

For many of us older folks, grandchildren come with the territory. Somebody said:

JUST WHEN A WOMAN THINKS HER WORK IS DONE . . .
SHE BECOMES A GRANDMOTHER.

Actually, my two granddaughters, Kandee and Tiffany, are more fun than work.

When Kandee was about five years old, I took her with me while speaking at a conference. During song time, all of the words to the songs were displayed on a big screen, and when I looked out in the audience, I saw little Kandee singing lustily as if she could read every word to every song. I knew (or at least I thought) that Kandee couldn't read yet and later I asked her how she knew all the words to the songs. "Oh, Grandma Barb," Kandee said excitedly, "I don't know any of them. I just sing 'watermelon-peanut butter' and it all comes out right!"

When Tiffany was six, she saw me on television, talking about one of my favorite bumper stickers: LIFE IS HARD AND THEN YOU DIE. When I got back, Tiffany was still there and she told me politely but firmly, "Grandma Barb, what you ought to say is, 'Life is hard, and then you GET to die and be with Jesus!' " I took Tiffany's advice and have been saying it that way ever since.

I like being a grandmother, but I try not to become too "grandmotherly." This poem sums it up pretty well for me:

THE VERSATILE AGE

The old rocking chair is empty today
Grandma is no longer in it.
She is off in her car to her office or shop
And buzzes around every minute.

You won't see her trundling off early to bed
From her place in a warm chimney nook.
Her typewriter clickety-clacks through the night
For Grandma is writing a book.

Grandma ne'er takes a backward look
To slow her steady advancing
She won't tend the babies for you anymore
For Grandma is taking up dancing.

Source unknown

## Growing Old with Mr. Wumphee

The other day I saw a cartoon picturing a wife sitting at one end of the sofa reading a magazine while her hubby slumped on the other end, fast asleep. The wife said: "Carl, if we're going to grow old together, you're going to have to slow up and wait for me."

That made me smile for two reasons: It was cute and I'm glad I don't have to say something like that to Bill. I'd say we're growing old together at just about an equal pace, even though I'm the sanguine and Mr. Wumphee is the pure melancholy. (In case you're wondering why I call Bill Mr. Wumphee, years ago he gave me the nickname "Cumphee." I needed a nickname for him and I came up with Wumphee, which doesn't mean anything, but at least it rhymes with Cumphee!)

I like dashing around, getting excited, and having FUN, while Bill is more dignified and deliberate about life. You can imagine his chagrin one night when we got into an elevator near the top floor of a big, new, fancy hotel, and I decided it might be fun to stop at every floor on the way down—to see if each one had the same decor, I guess. So I ran my finger down the panel, touching EVERY NUMBER!

Sure enough, the elevator obeyed my programming and stopped at EVERY FLOOR. People would get on and wonder what in the world was happening as the elevator stopped at every floor, the doors would open, and no one would get on— or off.

Bill sort of scrunched back in the corner and pretended he wasn't with me. No one knew I had done it, of course, so I acted as perplexed as the rest of them. "Wonder what's wrong with the system?" I said loudly. "You would think a brand new hotel could do better than THIS!" Everybody on board probably thought they just hadn't ironed out all the bugs yet. I wasn't about to tell them anything DIFFERENT!

We made twenty-two stops in all before we got to the lobby. It was a special memory for me, but a nightmare for Bill. Even now, when we get on an elevator where there are lots and lots of buttons, he starts to groan when I make a gesture as if I'm going to make one big SWIPE down the panel and repeat what happened that night. I'm only joking, of course, because I AM trying to become more mature as I get older.

Poor Bill. He doesn't think a lot of my crazy antics are much fun at all. His idea of a good time is getting the bumps on the bread matched when he makes sandwiches, or putting all the glasses in the cupboard according to correct size. He also likes categorizing the Spatula Ministries' bills each month in separate folders.

Just last Sunday we went over to a neighbor's house and Bill immediately noticed the telephone cord was all kinked up. So he spent fifteen minutes getting it totally straightened out and smooth again. Bill quickly spotted the messy cord because he's always straightening out ours. After I've been on the phone all day, it can get pretty twisted—and me along with it!

Bill is usually much better at remembering things and details than I am. He keeps track of the Spatula checking account and always balances the checkbook to the penny. In contrast, I handle our personal checking account, and if I come within a twenty-dollar difference from the bank statement, I feel I did great!

Bill may be a master at details, but tact and diplomacy aren't two of his strong points. One day I put on a new dress because I was going out to tape a TV program. Just before I left for the studio, I asked him if I looked okay. Bill said, "You look real nice and MATRONLY!"

Now, I know I AM a matron, but I don't want to be told I LOOK like one! I went back in the bedroom, changed into something else, and vowed never to wear the "matronly" dress again. Bill will probably never know how much that observation cost him. He made the remark innocently enough, I guess, because to him matronly means dignified or conservative, but to ME it means I'm ready for support hose.

## Could Rubber Peanuts Be THAT Delicious?

Usually I have been the practical joker in the family, but every now and then Bill gets into the act, too, sometimes without realizing it. Several years ago—when Bill's mom was still

# MY STAIR TREADS HAVE

# STARTED TO WEAR OUT

HADLEY ROBERTSON

SO I'VE PLACED A RAISIN IN
THE MIDDLE OF EACH AS A
REMINDER TO USE THE
OUTSIDE EDGES FOR AWHILE.

alive—he would often drive over to spend the day with her and his dad. Because she loved all kinds of nuts, I would send along a casserole or some other dish made with nuts. Sometimes I'd just send a dish of assorted nuts for Grandma to nibble on.

It was around April Fools' Day and Bill was headed over to see his mom, so I decided to have some fun. I found a small package of RUBBER peanuts and sprinkled them in with the dish of mixed nuts I was sending over. I thought it would be cute to have Grandma try one of the rubber peanuts and get a chuckle out of the joke I had played on her.

I waited all day for Bill to come back home to tell me what happened when Grandma tried the rubber peanuts. He walked in and put the empty dish on the table and I asked, "Where are all the rubber peanuts? What did your mom say when she tried one?"

"I don't know," Bill said.

"What do you mean you don't know? All the rubber peanuts are GONE!"

"Well," said Bill, "I'm not sure what happened. I gave Mom the bowl and Dad and I went out grocery shopping. When we came back, the bowl was empty!"

"You mean she ate ALL the peanuts?" I asked in dismay.

Bill just sort of smiled and said, "When I asked her what she had done with the rubber peanuts, she just said, 'What rubber peanuts?'"

I know some of these crazy stories I tell are pretty hard to believe sometimes. But I promise you I am not making this up! And if you think about it, it is conceivable that Grandma had eaten the rubber peanuts without even noticing. After all, she was eighty-seven at the time and still had all her own teeth. She always ate everything I sent over eagerly and with gusto. Anyway, Grandma lived almost ten more years, so the rubber peanuts couldn't have been the cause of her passing!

Mr. Wumphee usually accompanies me on my out-of-town speaking trips. Recently we were in Spokane and somebody called Bill up on the stage to say a few words. Bill claims that he hates to do that, but he always seems to have a great time, and so does the audience.

On that particular occasion, he said, "I have only one observation to make. I think that when you're married, you should be best friends, and that's why I'm happy to wear this 'Best Friends' button." And then he held up a button he had gotten at the conference with a picture of BOTH of us on it. So, while we're very different, we're very good for each other. We don't mind getting older, because we each have a best friend to do it with!

## Plenty of Growing Up Left to Do

I'm still hoping to figure out what I want to be when I grow up. Every now and then I ask myself, *How could I have possibly come so far and still have so far to go?* A good goal—and I invite you to make it your goal, too—is to be what this poem calls a "mid-life grownup":

> We aren't as self-centered as we used to be.
> We're not as judgmental—or just plain dumb.
> Adulthood has come, and it brings
> (Along with deepening laugh lines)
> Some sweet compensations.
>
> We aren't as self-righteous as we used to be.
> We've learned to tell the real from the tinsel and fluff.
> Growing up is tough, but it brings
> (Along with receding gum lines)
> Some sweet compensations.
>
> We aren't as self-pitying as we used to be.
> We know what we like—in work, in play.
> There's still more growing ahead. May it bring
> (Along with a softened jaw line)
> Some sweet compensations.
>
> Source unknown

One of my favorite actresses is Angela Lansbury, who has made "Murder, She Wrote" almost a way of life for thousands of people across the country. I heard Angela interviewed on "Donahue" recently, and one woman in the audience said that her mother would not even answer the phone during the hour that "Murder, She Wrote" was broadcasting.

As I sat there admiring how Angela conducted herself on the "Donahue" show, I thought, *Angela Lansbury is my idea of what I want to be when I get to be her age.* But then I realized I AM her age—along with Shirley Temple, Mickey Mouse, and Erma Bombeck!

## Be Childlike, Not Childish

To be honest, I suppose I'm more interested in becoming more childlike than becoming more mature. Note that I said child*like*, not child*ish*. Almost ten years ago I wrote a page for the September issue of our *Love Line* newsletter and said:

> Well, the kids are all starting school and most of us who are mothers at the age between estrogen and death don't have to think about back-to-school sales or packing lunches with "ants-on-a-log" (celery stuffed with peanut butter and raisins sprinkled on top). September brings to my mind kids and how I won't be one again or have one again. But I know there is still a child IN ME who helps me rediscover the sense of wonder and spontaneity that so many grownups lose along the way. I would like to share some thoughts about ways to KEEP that child in us alive!
>
> They say when you turn 40 life begins . . . but it begins to DISINTEGRATE! When you turn FIFTY, you really are in the stage between estrogen and death, and we are continually re-minded that it takes more time and energy to just HOLD THE LINE! So what if the aging process happens . . . it hits EVERY-ONE! One neat thing is IT ISN'T YOUR FAULT! How wonder-ful to know that this situation isn't something we did to have it come on us! No blame-game here!

When I counsel mothers who are still "in the twilight zone," I encourage them to inject some humor in their lives. Our youth may be lost or fading, but by letting ourselves be a child again, we can tap into a boundless fountain within us. So learn to laugh. Kids laugh out of sheer joy . . . no big reason. Quit taking yourself so seriously. Do some fun things just because you want to be impulsive and adventurous. If your life is so planned out you can't be flexible, you have forgotten how to be like a child. We know that "hardening of the attitudes" is a SURE sign of advancing age.

So hang loose in every area you can. Listen to that long-lost child and catch the small, simple blessing, often fleeting. Remember the sweetness of Indian Summer, the sharp fragrance of orange peel so reminiscent of Christmas, the surprise in children's eyes as they see the silvery sparkle on a frosty morning.

Reflect on shared joys and rewarding friendships. Remember the sapphire sky and the sunset's afterglow? To see and appreciate these things is like seeing the world through the eyes of a child. BE A CHILD AGAIN! Let yourself recapture that childlike essence. It's wonderful to be CHILDLIKE, just don't confuse it with being CHILDISH. There IS a difference.

Almost ten years after writing those words, I find them to be even truer than ever. As Bonnie Prudden says:

> YOU CAN'T TURN BACK THE CLOCK,
> BUT YOU CAN WIND IT UP AGAIN.

For me, being childlike means accepting the age spots, wrinkles, and other outward signs of aging with as much grace and style as possible. After all, it's better to be over the hill than under it!

As for the battle of the bulge, KEEP AT IT BECAUSE HELP IS ON THE WAY. According to the experts, an anti-fat pill is in the works. It will be a few more years before it is available, but they are trying to develop ways to fool the brain into thinking the body is fatter than it really is. Somehow, this pill will tell you that your body has had enough food and you won't be craving that midnight or midday snack. Can you imagine what it would be like to be able to take your anti-fat pill each day? And why not? They have pills for just about any other ailment or condition.

So keep pushing that beach ball down. In a couple of years it may be gone forever!

**Splish/Splash . . .**

> I SWAM 10 LAPS
> I RAN 3 MILES
> I BIKED 7 MILES . . .
> IT'S BEEN A GOOD YEAR!

*   *   *   *   *   *

Probably the only great thing about pantyhose is that every time you wash them they go back to their original shape. I look at that puckered, starved, withered six inches of nylon and feel reborn. God has given me a second chance to pack it in.

*   *   *   *   *   *

> YOU ARE WHAT YOU EAT
> SO I EAT ONLY RICH FOOD.

*   *   *   *   *   *

When short hemlines came back in fashion, a woman dug an old miniskirt out of her closet. She tried it on, but couldn't figure out what to do with the other leg.

*   *   *   *   *   *

> THE EASIEST WAY TO GET A HEALTHY BODY
> IS TO MARRY ONE.

*   *   *   *   *   *

I'M NOT RICH AND FAMOUS . . .
BUT I DO HAVE
PRICELESS GRANDCHILDREN.

\*     \*     \*     \*     \*     \*

### WHAT TO COUNT

Don't count how many years you've spent,
Just count the good you've done;
The times you've lent a helping hand,
The friends that you have won.
Count your deeds of kindness,
The smiles, not the tears;
Count all the pleasures that you've had,
But never count the years!

Source unknown

\*     \*     \*     \*     \*     \*

MY MIND WORKS LIKE LIGHTNING . . .
ONE BRILLIANT FLASH AND THEN IT'S GONE AGAIN!

\*     \*     \*     \*     \*     \*

NEVER TRY TO GUESS YOUR WIFE'S SIZE. JUST BUY HER
ANYTHING MARKED "PETITE" AND HOLD ON TO THE
RECEIPT.

\*     \*     \*     \*     \*     \*

THERE IS NO BETTER EXERCISE FOR THE HEART
THAN REACHING DOWN AND LIFTING SOMEONE UP.

\*     \*     \*     \*     \*     \*

MY MEMORY IS EXCELLENT. THERE ARE ONLY THREE
THINGS I CAN'T REMEMBER. I CAN'T REMEMBER FACES,

I CAN'T REMEMBER NAMES, AND NOW I HAVE FORGOT-
TEN THE THIRD THING.

\*   \*   \*   \*   \*   \*

AVENGE YOURSELF:
LIVE LONG ENOUGH TO BE A PROBLEM
TO YOUR CHILDREN.

\*   \*   \*   \*   \*   \*

Even to your old age and gray hairs
I am he, I am he who will sustain you.
I have made you and I will carry you;
I will sustain you and I will rescue you.
                              Isa. 46:4, NIV

# Motherhood Is Not for Wimps

*Cleaning your house*
*while your kids are still growing,*
*is like shoveling the walk*
*before it stops snowing[1]*

Every May, I dedicate our *Love Line* newsletter to moms because:

1. It's Mother's Day.
2. They deserve it.

At least once a year I think moms should be able to wake up and realize:

I'M NOT JUST A HOUSEWIFE,
I'M A DOMESTIC GODDESS![2]

I know a lot of mothers are opting for careers outside the home, but that doesn't do away with their "housewife" chores. I have worked off and on over the years, myself, but I always came home to the housewife work at the end of the day, which seldom made me feel like a domestic goddess. I ran across an article entitled, "Who Mothers Mothers?" That's a provocative question. It certainly isn't your husband. He has his own schedule and responsibilities. Some younger moms say their husbands are helping more at home, but they seem to be the minority. Even in the so-called "enlightened nineties," *the family still depends on Mom to make it tick*. I like the unknown poet's verse that describes a scene many moms are all too familiar with:

Of Detergent and Determination

Some may climb Mount Everest
    in search of thrills galore,
But I scale peaks that rival it
    just past my laundry door:
Slopes of socks and underwear,
    sheer cliffs of shirts and pants—
Oh, yes, I live in mortal fear
    of a laundry avalanche!

Who mothers mothers? It certainly isn't the kids. THEY are the ones who get up every morning determined to prove that motherhood is definitely not for wimps.

Then who really mothers mothers? Other mothers, of course! Only a mom understands when another mom needs a break from car-pool crazies, a listening ear, or just the discretion to look the other way when the kids go temporarily insane at the supermarket check-out counter.

At Spatula, we try to put hurting moms in touch with other hurting moms so they can find comfort, help, growth—and IMPROVEMENT. Husbands are protectors and breadwinners, but they aren't always equipped to help when you're hurting. Often, it's best to find a solid Christian WOMAN friend to listen to you ventilate and release your pent-up emotions. Then you will find that you will begin to get WELL. You will be comforted. IT REALLY WORKS THIS WAY!

## You Never Get Over Being a Mother

Where would we be without our kids? Maybe Maui? The Caribbean? Acapulco? For years I've collected quips on the "challenge" of motherhood (and fatherhood, too, for that matter). Here are just a few samples:

THE SECRET OF DEALING SUCCESSFULLY
WITH A CHILD IS NOT TO BE ITS PARENT.

\*   \*   \*   \*   \*   \*

THE JOY OF MOTHERHOOD:
WHAT A WOMAN EXPERIENCES WHEN ALL THE CHILDREN
ARE FINALLY IN BED.

\*   \*   \*   \*   \*   \*

A MOTHER OF THREE NOTORIOUSLY UNRULY KIDS
WAS ASKED, "IF YOU HAD IT TO DO ALL OVER AGAIN,
WOULD YOU HAVE CHILDREN?"
"YES," SHE REPLIED, "BUT NOT THE SAME ONES."

\*   \*   \*   \*   \*   \*

THE SMARTEST ADVICE ON RAISING CHILDREN
IS TO ENJOY THEM WHILE THEY ARE STILL ON YOUR SIDE.

\*   \*   \*   \*   \*   \*

JUST WHEN YOUR KIDS ARE FIT TO LIVE WITH
THEY'RE LIVING WITH SOMEONE ELSE.

\*   \*   \*   \*   \*   \*

Obviously, all these jokes and jibes about being a parent only cover up what everybody knows is true: Moms AREN'T wimps, but they ARE softies who will do ANYTHING for their children. You can get over a lot of things, but you never get over being a mother.

For example, my youngest son, Barney, who lives near Carson City, Nevada, with his wife, Shannon, and their

# I try to take just one day at a time...

# but lately several days have attacked me at once.

daughters, Kandee and Tiffany, flew down to Florida recently to get some training he would use in his curb and landscaping business. The day Barney left, a radio news flash said there was a heavy infestation of killer bees in Florida and I immediately remembered that Barney is allergic to bee stings. My first thought was, *I wonder if he remembered to take his bee-sting kit—the one he carries in his truck when he is out working. I bet he didn't take it with him.*

I could hardly wait to get to a phone to call Shannon to learn what happened. Shannon didn't answer, so I began praying, "Oh, Lord, protect him because if he gets stung and doesn't have the kit and doesn't get to a hospital—I mean—he could DIE! I realize You already know this, Lord, but You also know

I'm his mother and I can't help but remind You of these things now and then."

Here I was, praying about my thirty-two-year-old son who hadn't lived at home for fourteen years, and I was still worrying about whether or not he was carrying his bee-sting kit!

Finally, I just said, "God, You'll have to protect him and put Your arms around him because I can't. If he doesn't have the kit and gets stung . . . well, he can get to a hospital to be helped."

It turned out that Barney had not taken the kit with him, but he didn't get stung by a single bee. Did the Lord protect him because of my prayer? I'd like to think so—at least that I gave Him a little nudge. God understands that you never get over being a mother. You can't resign. There's no way out. You worry about your kids—and you worry about your kids some more. Having a child is like getting a life sentence in prison with no hope of parole. You are a mother until they put you in your grave.

## Why Do Mothers Cry?

As a mom, I have shed my share of tears over my kids, just as you have. I love a column someone sent me on why mothers cry. According to the author, when he was a little boy he found his mother humming her favorite song, "An Irish Lullaby," while tears trickled down her cheeks.

> "Why are you crying?" he asked his mom.
> "Because I'm a mother," she told him.
> "I don't understand," he said.
> His mom just hugged him tightly and said, "You never will."
> Later the boy asked his father why Mother seemed to cry for no reason.
> "All mothers cry for no reason," was all his dad could say.
> The little boy grew up, still wondering why mothers cry, so he finally put in a call to God and when he got Him on the line, God said, "You see, Stan, when I made mothers, they had to be special. I made their shoulders strong enough to carry the

weight of the world. I gave them the inner strength to endure childbirth and the rejection that eventually comes from their children.

"I gave them a hardiness that allows them to keep going when everyone else gives up, and to take care of their families through sickness and fatigue without complaining.

"I gave them the sensitivity to love their children under all circumstances, and no matter how badly they are hurt. This same sensitivity helps them to make a child's boo-boo feel better, and helps them share a son's teen-age anxieties.

"I gave them a tear to shed. It's theirs exclusively to use whenever it's needed. It's their only weakness. It's a tear for mankind."[3]

Here is another story about a mother's tears that one of my friends sent me:

There once was a procession of children marching in heaven. Each child held a lighted candle, and as they marched along they sang. Their faces shone with happiness. But one little girl stood all alone.

"Why don't you join us, little girl?" one happy child asked.

"I can't," she replied."Every time I light my candle, my mother puts it out with her tears."

## The Pitfalls of Parenting

Two common pitfalls for a lot of parents, especially moms, are:

1. Being afraid to let them grow up, try things, stumble over a few rocks in the road.

2. Feeling guilty when their kids do stumble, have problems, rebel—or worse.

The first pitfall—wanting to make life perfectly smooth for our kids—is the "overparenting" syndrome, or what Erma Bombeck calls TMM (Too Much Mother). A mother should be like a blanket . . . keeping the children warm but not SMOTHERING them.

From the moment they can start toddling off on their own, our kids want to separate from us. At age two, they tell us, "I do it MYSELF." By the time they hit the teen-age years, kids are practically at war with their parents over what they think they can or can't do.

From the parents' point of view, kids think they're far more capable than they really are. Furthermore, if they'd just act more RESPONSIBLE, perhaps mothers wouldn't have to worry so much. Maybe you've heard some of the following, and probably you've even used one or two of them yourself:

THE WORLD ACCORDING TO PARENTS

- "Bring me the change."
- "Call us when you get there."
- "I hope I'm alive when your kids turn sixteen."
- "Stop whining and eat it, NOBODY LIVES FOREVER."
- "If you break your leg, don't come running to me."
- "You WILL have fun."
- "Do it to make your mother happy."
- "Wait until your dad gets home."

Source unknown

Just as the mother bird shoves her fledglings out of the nest and the mother bear boots her little cubs out of the den to start foraging for themselves, so we human moms need to let our kids strike out on their own. As one writer says, "We . . . cling to our children as if we are afraid to trust God with them!"[4]

I'm not suggesting that we start neglecting our kids—far from it. But I think we should start letting go of them a lot earlier. One way to make life *hard* for our kids is to make life too *soft* for them.

In chapter 3 I talked about letting go of Larry and finally being able to pray, "Whatever, Lord," when he had appeared to stray so far from God and the foundation we had given him.

*children are a great comfort in your old age...*
*and they help you reach it faster too !*

*Children are a gift of the Lord... Psa 127:3*

Even better, however, is for moms to pray, "Whatever, Lord," when their kids are little, realizing that, "God has a Will and a Way for our children, and the road ahead may be rough. He foreknew them just as he foreknew us. At some point God and child must meet and establish their own relationship."[5]

## Guilt Quickly Turns into a Deep Cesspool

The other pitfall that turns into a cesspool for so many parents is guilt, the emotion Erma Bombeck calls the "gift that keeps on giving." A constant theme running through many letters I receive concerns the guilt and sense of failure parents feel when a child rebels and rejects the family's values. As one mother wrote to me:

> I know there are many hurting parents out there and we are not unique. We want to stand firm and be faithful, we want to be happy! We don't want to choose misery [but] we have failed.

Guilt becomes particularly overwhelming when parents hear their son or daughter say, "Mom, I'm gay—I have been almost since I can remember." A mother whose son grew up in the church and at one time attended a Christian college with a goal to work with young people in counseling against drugs wrote to say this after she learned he was gay:

> Barbara, I thought I knew the answers before it became *my son*. It's a secret I carry ashamedly; it hurts me so to have my only two children so far apart.
>
> How do these things happen? Why? What can I do? . . . I'm desperate . . . Help me to help my child!

Another mother wrote after talking to me on the phone about her son, whose homosexual lifestyle was affecting her two younger children, as well as the whole family. As heartbreaking as it was, she and her husband had to ask him to leave because of the damage he was doing in their home. They couldn't let the sins of one person destroy their whole family.

At first he was angry and she heard very little from him, but he did spend Christmas with the family and they got along fairly well, mainly because she and her husband didn't question or judge him. Their relationship is still strained, however, and she writes:

> What has been hard for my husband and me to understand is why he is so involved in this. We brought him up in the belief of God and salvation. My husband does not feel much now but anger and relief that he is out of the home, but I have to pray daily for God to give me the strength to trust Him. I placed my son in His arms, but yet I keep feeling anxious each day. I find myself checking the newspaper, or scanning the streets when I'm in the area where I think he might be.
>
> P.S. Any tips on how to not feel so guilty? Especially since we asked him to leave, I feel like a hypocrite, even though circumstances forced us to do so. But I feel so badly. One part of me wants to bring him home and take care of him.

Another mother wrote to tell me of her son's divorce and his moving back home, where he now lives with his parents and "drinks too much." His two little girls visit every other weekend. The mother's letter continued:

> He was raised in a Christian home and therefore I carried such guilt, knowing I had failed somewhere. God surely led me to that bookstore on a day when I needed to hear the words of joy found in your book . . . It has opened my eyes to so much. I know I must love him and let God change him. We parents feel that changing them is our job. It's not. It's God's.

This mom has gotten the message! It's our job to love our kids; it's God's job to bring conviction.

When a child strays away or adopts a destructive lifestyle, parents automatically ask, "What did I do wrong?"

"Nothing most other parents didn't do, too," I tell them. "Remember that God calls us to be faithful; He doesn't call us to be successful."

Parents can only do their best—no more, no less. Even what they do or don't do isn't the final cause of how their children turn out. For years the behavioral school of psychology said that the child's environment has the main influence on a child's development, but recently more psychologists are saying that genetics are the key factor. Since even the experts don't agree on this, perhaps it is a balance or blend of both.

The point is, parents don't have to accept the blame for their kids' choices. There is no need to wear a guilt quilt. Instead, wrap yourself in God's comfort blanket and remember two things:

1. IF THERE IS NO CONTROL
   THERE IS NO RESPONSIBILITY.
2. GOD HAS THE FINAL WORD
   ON WHAT HAPPENS TO YOUR CHILD.

Also remember that there is an abundance of God's grace for us all. Grace can cover even your shame and guilt, no matter how badly you feel.

Because we use and reuse a lot of cassette tapes, Bill bought me a fabulous invention called a tape eraser. You slip a tape in it, and when it comes out the tape is completely BLANK. Something inside completely erases the tape so it can be used again for new material.

This machine is only about as big as a tape, itself, and works like a charm. I pasted a little cartoon on the outside—a little girl asking, "Dear God, when You forgive, do You use an eraser?"

Sometimes I sit and erase hundreds of tapes for reuse, and I think of that wonderful land of beginning again where we are forgiven our sins and cleansed from all unrighteousness (1 John 1:9). Calvary covers ALL my past sins. Jesus took on all our guilt and wiped out all charges against us. Just as my little cassette tape eraser can cleanse a tape and make it fit for use like brand new, so can God cleanse my heart and make me fresh and clean.

And the most important thing is to remember that God's "tape eraser" is always ready when we fail or make mistakes. You may have heard the story of the minister who was entertaining some important Christian leaders. His wife had made a lovely, formal meal using her finest crystal, silver, and china. Their seven-year-old son was at the table, and as he reached for something he knocked over his water goblet. It was a tense, silent moment. The boy had fear written all over his face as he stared at his father, who was looking toward him intently.

Then the minister reached out and dumped his own goblet, splashing water all over the place as his son had done. Following suit, each guest did the same. It was as if they all understood that the father didn't want the son to feel guilty alone. He was willing to identify with his son at this embarrassing moment.

This homey little story is only a tiny glimpse of how grace works. Yet it helps us picture how God identifies with us in all our suffering and our failures. And as God identifies with us,

HE SPLASHES HIS GRACE ALL OVER US. There is more than enough for everyone.

## Today's Experiences Are Tomorrow's Memories

Instead of smother-mothering your kids and then feeling guilty about their poor choices, take every opportunity to make good memories instead. Overmothering means focusing so tightly on the child that neither one of you has room to breathe. Making good memories calls for focusing on BOTH of you. You do things to make good memories for the child, but you also do things that make them for YOU.

In chapter 2, I described the bittersweet memories that occur when sorrow invades a family. But there are also the PLEASANT or FOND memories that remind you of dreams and plans and good times that are and always will be part of you. Remember:

THE MEMORY IS A WONDERFUL TREASURE CHEST
FOR THOSE WHO KNOW HOW TO PACK IT.

It's not surprising that so many middle-aged men, in particular, walked out of the movie *Field of Dreams* with tears in their eyes. The film, about a man who turns an Iowa cornfield into a baseball diamond complete with lights, touched a nerve across America because it reminded so many men of the days when they played baseball and perhaps dreamed of making it all the way to the majors.

For all of us, today's experiences are tomorrow's memories. In looking back over more than fifty years to things that happened when I was a small girl, the indelible memories are there, reminding me of who I am and where I came from.

I started singing when I was about three years old and, because my dad was a church music director, he gave me all kinds of opportunities. For example, Billy Sunday, the Billy Graham of that day, came to our town to preach. My dad stood me up on a chair so I could reach the microphone and sing during Billy Sunday's meetings, which were held in a big tent where the ground was covered with wood shavings and sawdust. When folks talk about the "sawdust trail" today, I know what that means because I was there. I can still smell those meetings in my memory whenever I'm around freshly cut lumber. And I still remember some of the songs I sang. One was:

> GOD CAN SEE EACH FALLING TEAR;
> HE SEES THE HEART THAT'S SAD AND DREAR.
> HE KNOWS THE PATH THAT'S FULL OF FEAR;
> DON'T GIVE UP FOR HE IS NEAR.

The audience would join with me to sing another song that went like this:

> Everybody happy, SAY AMEN!
> Everybody happy, SAY AMEN!
> Praise the Lord for what He's done,
> Praise the Lord for victories won,
> Everybody happy, SAY AMEN!

The audience would sing the first part of the line and I would chirp, "SAY AMEN!"—loudly and with much gusto, of course.

Some missionaries to China visited our church and taught me to sing a song to the tune of "Bringing in the Sheaves." What I thought I heard them teaching me sounded like this:

> Don you ting wah chee . . .
> Don you ting wah chee . . .
> Hi lo ling tum fi low,
> Don you ting wah chee.

Rattling off these words for the congregation usually got lots of applause. After all, here I was, a little kid, singing a song in Chinese—very impressive! A few years later, I sang the same thing for some REAL Chinese friends and they didn't understand a word I said!

My memories include my bedtime routine. I would sit on my dad's lap and he would rock me as we would listen to the "Amos and Andy" radio show together. It always ended at 7:30 and then I knew it was time for bed.

Sometimes my sister, who was eight years older than I was, would have to take care of me, and she would want me to go to bed earlier so she could get me out of her way. She would set the clock an hour or so AHEAD; but I always knew, until I heard the closing strains of "Amos and Andy," it wasn't time for bed, no matter how many times she moved the clock ahead!

## Parents Are Writing a Lasting Record

Parents can write many things on the heart of a child, sometimes without realizing it. Often what you are as a parent—your integrity, your character—will make a memory your child will never forget.

When I was about ten years old, I found an advertisement somewhere that said if I could sell one hundred jars of Cloverine Salve I would earn a bicycle. Somehow I got my mother to order the 100 jars, anticipating how I would sell them all and get myself a BIKE. Cloverine Salve, according to the ad, was for everything—cows' udders, washing machines, sore cuts, squeaky door hinges, you name it. Today I guess it would be a cross between Vaseline and WD-40.

I can still remember going from door to door, pleading with folks to buy my Cloverine Salve. It was winter in Michigan and biting cold. The snow swirled around me as I trudged from house to house. I had packed several jars of the salve in a sack and just carrying it was burdensome. My galoshes were wet inside where the snow had spilled over the tops. My socks got wet and my feet were cold. And every time I got to a door I would have to remove my woolly mitten in order to push the doorbell. Soon my fingers were like icicles.

Despite all of my efforts to tell folks how useful the salve was, nobody wanted to buy it. If you have ever lived in a cold climate like Michigan and trudged through snow and slush with the biting cold piercing right through your clothes, you know how DETERMINED I was to sell that salve. But all I kept getting was "No, thank you"; then I'd pick up my sack and move on down the block to the next rejection, always hoping that I could earn the shiny bike shown in that advertisement.

I would come home after my "sales trips," totally discouraged because my sack of salve had not diminished. And our garage was still STACKED with boxes of Cloverine Salve. My longed-for bike seemed to be just a broken dream. I had managed to get rid of only a few jars by selling them to relatives who loved me anyway and felt sorry for me. But I was nowhere near selling them all, and that was the deal, if I was to get that new bike.

Just as I was about to give up, my dad came to my rescue. He had seen me come in so many times with teeth chattering, clothes sopping wet, face red and chapped from the biting cold. He knew it was an overwhelming task and that no one wanted the salve because it was the depression and no one had any extra money for things like that.

But as a caring dad, he wanted my dream to come true, so he purchased all the remaining jars of Cloverine Salve from me, saying, "Oh, we'll eventually use them all up." Thrilled to pieces, I watched him make out the money order to pay for the salve and then I ran to the corner mailbox to send it in.

For the next several weeks I waited with excited anticipation for a beautiful, shiny bike like the one pictured in the advertisement. I knew that soon I would be riding that bike, pedaling around the neighborhood with my hair blowing in the wind. I envisioned streamers coming from the handlebars and, of course, a nice loud jingling bell. What excitement . . . what anticipation for a little girl who at last would have her VERY OWN BIKE!

Finally, the bike did arrive in the mail. The only problem was, it was made of aluminum, about fifteen inches long and six inches high! It was nothing more than a TOY! My disappointment was twice as great as my anticipation had been and I started to cry bitterly. I had expected a nice, new, shiny, red bike with a bell and streamers—everything I had dreamed of. Instead, I had gotten a cheap toy that you could hold in two hands.

My dad saw my tear-streaked face and a few hours later he had me in the car and we went shopping for a new bright, shiny red bicycle. This was back when times were hard and people were hurting from the depression and luxuries like new bikes were not readily available. But we shopped and shopped and finally found that "just-right" bike.

I'm sure that Dad and Mom went without other things in order to get me that bike, which I treasured and rode for years. Once in a while I see an ad for Cloverine Salve—in some old farm catalog or on a poster in an antique shop. Then the memory of that day when my dad took me out to buy that new bike floods back and splashes me with joy.

## The Things We Never Forget

When we look back at childhood, there are "things we will never forget." Some of the ideas I remember most fondly are:

1. The simple joys of picking wild violets or gathering hickory nuts with a grandparent.
2. Being ill, missing school, and getting strawberry ice cream.
3. The first time I slept in a tent.
4. Holidays with all the relatives joking, laughing, and eating.
5. Catching "lightning bugs" and putting them in a bottle.
6. Watching a favorite TV show with the family.

This morning I flipped on our television set and heard the nostalgic tune that was the theme song for the "Little Rascals" program from more than thirty years ago. I sat transfixed as I watched Spanky, Darla, and Alfalfa cavorting across the screen with their songs and antics. And I thought back to when I had heard boyish chuckles and outright belly laughs as my children had delighted in all the "Little Rascals'" mischief.

Watching that rerun was a special time, as the Rascals drove an old, beat-up car down a winding street and Alfalfa sang off key. I enjoyed that time alone, remembering all the fun we had had on Saturday mornings. Then I realized those original "Little Rascal" days were long gone for me. And those little boys who laughed so uproariously were gone from our family room, too.

Instead, now I sat alone with memories of the laughter we had built into the walls of our home and our hearts. I suppose I could have become morbid about it, but instead I began to think of Philippians 4:8 and how important it is to think on things that are pure and good and also happy. (I'm sure Paul meant to put "happy" in there some place.) And so I captured in my mind the rollicking fun of Saturday mornings as our boys were growing up. I could almost smell the cereal with bananas they would devour as they watched their favorite TV characters—and we laughed and laughed together.

## The Memory of the Micro-Sweater

Today's experiences ARE tomorrow's memories, and I thank God I took time to make as many as possible. While Steve was still in high school, his girlfriend knitted him a beautiful light-green sweater, and when he came home with it, we all admired it because it was, indeed, lovely. He was so proud of that sweater, and he loved it more than anything else in his entire wardrobe.

But a day or two later, he came home from school all upset. He had spilled hot chocolate all over his sweater and was sure it was ruined. "Don't worry," I said, "I'll wash it for you and it will come out fine."

"Oh, no," he protested, "don't you touch it. You might SHRINK it!"

I just smiled at Steve's very explicit orders to leave his sweater alone, but after he left for school I did what any mother would do. I carefully washed the sweater, which came out looking as beautiful as ever. As I put it in his dresser drawer, a devious little thought crossed my mind. If there were only some way to make Steve think the sweater was ruined, and then have him find it clean and carefully folded and waiting in his drawer . . .

Later that day, as I was going to the market, I went by a store that sold Ken and Barbie dolls and all the accessories. Looking in the window, I was delighted to see a tiny, light-green sweater that perfectly matched Steve's in color, texture, and style! The only difference was that Steve's sweater was at least fifteen times larger! The tiny sweater in the window was the size of the palm of my hand and I knew I had to have it!

I went in and bought the micro-sweater and rushed home. With only a few minutes to spare before Steve was due home from school, I laid the tiny sweater on his bed. Then I went out to the kitchen to wait for Steve to come through the door. Sure enough, he was home in a few minutes, said his usual "Hi," and went right on by me to his room. I just kept humming and fixing dinner, but it didn't take long for Steve's howl of anguish to come down the hall.

"My sweater . . . it looks like a coaster! You RUINED it! I KNEW this would happen. You BOILED my sweater!"

I went to his room to see what all the ruckus was about (as if I didn't know). Desperately, Steve was trying to stretch the tiny sweater to make it larger, but it was no use. "Oh, yes," I said, "I tried to wash your sweater but I guess it must have shrunk . . ."

I let Steve writhe in anxiety for a few more seconds and then started to laugh. "Steve, do you really think that I would hurt something that meant so much to you?" I asked as I calmly opened his dresser drawer. There was the puffy green sweater, looking brand new and quite a bit larger than the miniature he was holding!

Steven's look of sheer delight as he took the real sweater out of the drawer is a memory I'll always treasure. I can still see his quick smile and twinkling eyes and hear his voice saying, "Awww, I KNEW you wouldn't REALLY hurt my sweater."

Steve thought I HAD ruined his sweater, but he still enjoyed the joke. Maybe he was just so relieved that he still had his sweater—but anyway, he started to laugh, too.

We kept the little green sweater on display for awhile and every time we saw it, we had another good chuckle together.

After Steve was killed and I began speaking to women's groups, I would take the little green sweater with me and display it as I shared my story. On occasion I have mentioned that the little green sweater was getting worn out because I have shown it so many hundreds of times. At least five women have made me duplicates of the sweater—same color, same style— but I still have the original one, too, which brings back precious memories every time I speak and share this story.

### Rockabye Barney on the Dryer Top

Recently I received a lovely cross-stitch, done by Barney's wife, Shannon, of the poem that appears on the next page.[6]

Shannon's cross-stitch not only thrilled me, but it stirred a lot of memories of that little boy I raised with love. The best memories are the ones that a mother treasures in her heart, the ones that no one knows about but her. One of my special memories of Barney is when he was a baby. He was born December 22 and I brought him home on Christmas morning in a big red stocking. Our special little gift developed colic and was constantly fussy, especially at night. I always said if Barney had been my FIRST, he definitely would have been my LAST.

Barney was the epitome of two of my favorite quips:

PEOPLE WHO SAY THEY SLEEP LIKE A BABY
USUALLY DON'T HAVE ONE.

L. J. Burke[7]

\*   \*   \*   \*   \*   \*

A PERFECT EXAMPLE OF MINORITY RULE
IS THE BABY IN THE HOUSE.

To get Barney to sleep, I would wrap him up tightly in a baby blanket, place him in a wicker laundry basket, then set

To my mom-in-love, ♡

You are the mother I received on the day I wed your son.

I just want to thank you, Mom, for the things you have done.

You have given me a gracious man with whom I share my life.

You are his lovely mother and I his adoring wife.

You used to pat his little head, and now I hold his hand.

You raised with love a little boy... then gave to me a man.

from your daughter-in-love

the basket on top of the clothes dryer and turn it on. (Please note that I set him ON the dryer, not IN the dryer.) Only then would Barney stop crying as the vibration and noise of the dryer lulled him to sleep.

Then I would set the timer on the dryer for 58 minutes (if I let it go an hour, the buzzer would wake him up). Then I would set my own alarm for a few minutes less than that and get that much shut-eye, myself. When my alarm went off, I would have to get up and re-set the dryer, hoping Barney would sleep another fifty-eight minutes. During his first six or seven months of life, that was the only way I could get any sleep at night. If I didn't leave Barney on the dryer and keep resetting that timer every hour, he would wake up screaming—and so would I.

The dryer trick worked until Barney was about seven months old; then he learned how to crawl OUT of the laundry basket and OFF the machine. By then, however, his colic was somewhat relieved, so we were able to sleep through the night.

Countless times I'd rock him to sleep, myself, as I sang songs and made up stories. And it worked, as the rhythm of the rocking would soothe him and quiet him down.

There is something almost magical about rocking. It begins in the womb with the child rocking as the mother moves about. Most of us were rocked as children, and it seems we never outgrow our need to be rocked.

Rocking soothes and comforts. I believe every home needs a rocking chair for use by the kids as well as the grownups. Older folks, grieving over the loss of friends who die or move away, often find comfort in rocking. Yes, rocking appeals to just about every age. At the Polly's Pie Shop restaurant near where we live, the waiting area is lined with about twenty rocking chairs. Bill and I find it so enjoyable just to sit and rock that we almost hate to have our turn come to be seated for lunch.

Now Barney, that little guy I rocked for countless hours, has grown up into a broad-shouldered, muscular man, over six feet tall and weighing nearly 180 pounds. Not long ago I received a rare treat from my son—something I treasure very much. On his way home from that trip to Florida (without his bee-sting kit), Barney wrote me a letter:

> Mom, I always have wanted to write you, but never had enough time to sit down and do it! So, I'm on the plane back from Florida and able to do so. I really appreciate you and love you, and know you love me also. There have been times in my life when I probably should have done something different or could have gotten into something else, but I am where I am today and happy because of you and Dad, who have given me and the girls and Shannon the love and the will and encouragement to hang tough!
>
> I love you so much, and am so proud of you. I just don't get to tell you enough how thankful I am for you and Dad. After being in business for myself for the last 2 years and dealing with employees and where they have come from and how they've been brought up, I can really appreciate how fortunate I was to have Dad and you.
>
> Love,
> Barney

As I finished Barney's letter, I had tears in my eyes, but I guess that's what motherhood is all about. As somebody said:

AT TIMES<br>
KIDS CAN BE A PAIN IN THE NECK<br>
WHEN THEY'RE NOT BEING A LUMP IN YOUR THROAT.

I'm glad I've had my share of both, and I hope you are, too!

## Splish/Splash . . .

LITTLE GIRL'S ESSAY ON PARENTS:

The trouble with parents is that they are so old when we get them, it's hard to change their habits.

*　*　*　*　*　*

A mom with little boy in tow met her pastor in the church hallway and said, "I was thinking of doing what *Hannah* did. As you will recall, she took her kid to the church and LEFT him there!"

\* \* \* \* \* \*

THE BEST WAY TO KEEP CHILDREN AT HOME
IS TO CREATE A PLEASANT ATMOSPHERE—
AND TO LET THE AIR OUT OF THEIR TIRES.

\* \* \* \* \* \*

Mother, talking to old college friend: "Remember, before I was married I had three theories about raising children? Well, now I have three children and no theories."

\* \* \* \* \* \*

RUN THE VACUUM OFTEN . . .
NOT TO CLEAN, BUT TO DROWN OUT THE KIDS.

\* \* \* \* \* \*

SCHOOL DAYS
CAN BE THE HAPPIEST DAYS OF YOUR LIFE . . .
PROVIDING THE CHILDREN ARE OLD ENOUGH TO GO.

\* \* \* \* \* \*

A SWEATER IS A GARMENT WORN BY A CHILD
WHEN HIS MOTHER FEELS CHILLY.

\* \* \* \* \* \*

YOU CAN GET CHILDREN
OFF YOUR LAP,
BUT YOU CAN NEVER GET THEM
OUT OF YOUR HEART.

\* \* \* \* \* \*

TO BE IN YOUR CHILDREN'S MEMORIES TOMORROW
YOU HAVE TO BE IN THEIR LIVES TODAY.

\*   \*   \*   \*   \*   \*

Don't keep on scolding and nagging your children, making
them angry and resentful. Rather, bring them up with the loving discipline the Lord himself approves, with suggestions and
godly advice. (Eph. 6:4, TLB)

# Oh, Lord, Let My Words Be Tender and Sweet, for Tomorrow I May Have to Eat Them!

*There is only one thing more painful
than learning from experience,
and that is not learning from experience.*

As I continue working with families who are torn by misunderstanding and confusion, an observation by Ashleigh Brilliant keeps coming to mind:

> IF ONLY I COULD RELATE TO
> THE PEOPLE I'M RELATED TO.[1]

So many parents and their grown children are caught in the same trap. They wish they could be close to one another, but they are separated by a huge canyon of disagreement, hurt feelings, or resentments. They try to send words to each other across that canyon, but so often the words don't arrive, or if they do, they convey the wrong message and the canyon grows even wider.

I know how this feels, and something that happened on Easter Sunday vividly reminded me of how wonderful it is to communicate in a warm, nonjudgmental way. Larry came over for dinner, and later he left to drive to his condo, about an hour away. Two hours later I received a phone call: "Mom! You'll never believe what happened to me after I left your place!"

I could tell from Larry's voice that something was definitely not right and, like any mother, I immediately considered panic. What in the world could Larry mean? And then he continued, "I had to stop for gas just before I got on the freeway, and while I was pumping gas, the nozzle went crazy and wouldn't shut off. By the time I finally got it stopped, gas was everywhere—in my hair, my eyes, and all over the new sweater you gave me."

"My goodness!" was all I could say. "What did you do then?"

"I went in the men's room, took off the sweater, and decided it was ruined; I just threw it in the trash barrel. My pants were soaked with gas, but I couldn't throw them away. So were my shoes. I paid for the gas, got back in the car, and drove home. I was glad nobody threw a cigarette out his window into mine or I would have exploded, I was just SOAKED with gasoline. I'm going to take a bath and try to get this smell off of me, and it looks as if I will have to throw away the rest of my clothes."

I told Larry I was glad he wasn't hurt or anything like that, and thanked him for calling. But after we hung up, I began thinking about that sweater. It was one I bought at Knott's Berry Farm and I had given it to him for Christmas. It was all cotton, a beautiful maroon color, and he had really liked it. I hated the thought of Larry's sweater winding up in the gas-station trash barrel.

Taking a big plastic sack with me (having faith I would ultimately find the sweater), I started up Fullerton Road, the most direct route to the freeway Larry would take to go on home. I stopped at the first gas station I found, got out, dragged my plastic sack with me, and asked the attendant, "Did a young man come in here a couple of hours ago for gas and have it spill all over him?"

The attendant looked at me a little strangely and said, "Naw, lady, I don't think we've EVER had that happen . . ."

I went through the same procedure as I worked my way up Fullerton Road, stopping at seven gas stations in all. Finally, I got to the eighth and last station and decided, *This MUST be it*, because I could see the freeway just a block ahead. I got out of my car with my plastic sack in hand and asked the question that by now had become a broken record. But this time a darling young man said, "Oh, man! Did we ever! We were so SORRY about what happened. He was saturated with gas!"

"That was my son," I told him. "He tells me he threw his sweater in your men's-room trash container, and I've come to try to get it back."

Sure enough, when the young man checked the restroom for me, he came back with the sweater in the plastic bag, matted, soaked in gas, and very smelly. I thanked him profusely and drove back home. Even with the sweater tied up in the plastic sack, my car was permeated with the smell of gasoline. When Bill heard I'd found it, he said, "Well, just leave it outside and it will air out. For Pete's sake, don't bring it in the house that way."

So I spread it out on some lawn furniture and left it there overnight hoping that most of the odor would be gone by morning. Believe it or not (remember, we live in Southern California), that night it poured. I went out the next morning and there was the sweater, all soggy now, not only with gas but with rain water. I decided I couldn't possibly take it to the cleaners in that condition.

## From Mom—With Love and Cologne

I wrung out as much moisture as I possibly could, and then proceeded to wash it at least three times in Woolite, plus three different fabric softeners. It came out soft, silky, almost WAXY smooth, and smelling perfectly fresh. Finding a nice box just the right size, I neatly folded the sweater, and for good measure tucked in several tissues well sprinkled with Bill's Royal Copenhagen aftershave and cologne. Now I was sure it would smell good when he opened it.

I thought how much fun it would have been if I had gotten the sweater to Larry on April 1, but the trouble was it was already April 1. There was still time to get to the UPS office though, and I sent it off, knowing he'd get it by April 2 at least. I could hardly wait until he called to tell me he had gotten back a sweater he never expected to see (or smell) again!

All week I kept waiting for Larry to call me about the sweater, but that call never came. It was now Friday, six days since I had found the sweater and cleaned it up. Before leaving to speak at a women's retreat in a valley just north of Los Angeles, I left a message on Larry's phone machine telling him that I would stop by on my way home on Sunday to take him to lunch at the Dorothy Chandler Pavilion near his condominium building.

That following Sunday I arrived in plenty of time and decided to go over to his condo to get him, so we could walk together to lunch. I rang the bell and Larry flung open the door. There he stood in all his maroon-sweater glory saying, "SMELL ME, MOM, SMELL ME!"

## Lunch Stirred Bittersweet Memories

We talked about the sweater all through lunch. He just couldn't believe that I could ever find it and, after finding it, get the gas smell out.

It was a delightful time. We laughed together easily, and I was thankful life was so good for us right now. As we sat in the Music Center restaurant enjoying ourselves, I remembered being in this same building on October 21, 1975, and feeling heartbroken because Larry wouldn't even speak to me. When I had learned about his homosexuality in June of that year, my rage had clashed with his angry reaction. He had left home and disappeared into the gay lifestyle. I had disappeared into our bedroom to count the roses on our wallpaper and slip deeper into depression.

We didn't hear anything from Larry. Then, in October, I saw a story in the *Los Angeles Times* saying the choral group Larry sang with would be performing at the Music Center. Accompanied by my sister, I went that night to hear the group sing and quickly spotted the smiling son I hadn't seen or heard from for four months. I never took my eyes off of Larry during the entire first half of the program. He was a bit thinner, perhaps, but he looked wonderful.

Our seats were close to the front, and as the house lights came on for intermission, Larry looked into the audience and saw me. Our eyes locked for just a second or two and then the curtain closed. I could hardly wait for intermission to be over so I could see him again during the second half of the program. I was hoping we could go backstage after the performance to congratulate him, but when the curtain went up Larry was not there. The place where he was supposed to stand and perform was empty. Apparently, he had grabbed his clothes in the dressing room and bolted out of the Music Center because he didn't want to see me at all!

Having Larry be so close and then losing him again made my depression even worse. Eventually it led me to the brink of suicide (see chapter 3). Larry was gone with no word for almost another eight months, and then, the very day after I came out of my suicidal doldrums by deciding to "nail him to the Cross" and say, "Whatever, Lord," he called and came home. I was glad, but there was still a nagging feeling that said, *This is not the time for real joy,* and I was right.

## Larry Decided to Disown Us

For the next three years, Larry stayed in touch while going to college at UCLA and living alone in an apartment near the campus. He would drop by and see us frequently, but we never talked about homosexuality. We just talked about surface things.

Then, in 1979, when my first book, *Where Does a Mother Go to Resign?* came out, Larry became sullen, unfriendly, and finally very angry. He let me know that he "had a lover," and while I did not go into a rage the way I had when I discovered his homosexuality, I was firm in saying that I didn't think homosexuality was God's best for anybody—especially my son. I would love him and pray for him. The porch light would always be on for him.

Larry did not listen. He hung up in anger, telling us that he was going to change his name and disown us because he never wanted to see us again. Sure enough, a few days later we received the official papers from the court that told us he had done just that. It was early in 1980. We would not hear from Larry for six years. I would go out to speak and share with other parents about how to handle pain and someone would ask, "How is your family doing now?"

My standard answer was: "Well, my two sons haven't risen from the dead, and I have a third son who has changed his name, disowned his family, told us he never wants to see us again, and has disappeared into the gay lifestyle. But who wants to hear a dreary story like that? I'm here to tell you not to give up hope, particularly when you're in a hopeless situation, because God only gives out the score on a life when the game is over—and the game isn't over YET with my kid."

One thing I have always stressed is that where there is no control, there is no responsibility. I couldn't change Larry. I couldn't fix him. I didn't even know where he WAS! But my joy lay in the fact that I knew I was living in a set of parentheses that would eventually be opened. Someday, one end of those parentheses would be kicked out and I would get on with my life. This whole thing hadn't come to stay; it was going to pass. I was living with a DEFERRED HOPE, but I knew it wouldn't be that way forever. As Proverbs says, "Hope deferred makes the heart sick; but when dreams come true at last, there is life and joy."[2]

I knew, even when trapped in those parentheses, that during a time of deferred hope, God still goes after the prodigal; God seeks out His own. He could end these parentheses any time He wanted to. I clung to the Proverb that says, "And you can also be very sure God will rescue the children of the godly."[3]

### "Mom, I Want to Bring You a Mother's Day Present"

I went on like that until just before Mother's Day 1986. Eleven years had passed since that day I had learned the truth about Larry's homosexuality; then came a shocking phone call. It was Larry, who said he wanted to bring me a "Mother's Day present." I confess all kinds of thoughts flashed into my mind—most of them bad. Was he bringing home his lover to tell us they were going to get married? Even the unthinkable crossed my mind: AIDS!

Fear paralyzed me. What could Larry want to bring me after all this time—all this estrangement? Bill could tell I was talking to Larry, and, sensing my hesitation, he said, "Tell him to come home." I did, and within an hour Larry arrived. He was supposed to be bringing me a present, but there was no package in his hand. It turned out he didn't need a package. What he had to give us was far better.

Larry came in, sat down, and with big tears in his eyes he asked us to forgive him for the eleven years of pain he had caused us. He had attended a Bill Gothard Advanced Seminar and had felt such conviction he had gone home to burn all the evidence of the old lifestyle and become clean in God's sight. There had been real restoration to God in his life and now he wanted to be restored to us, as well!

The word "restore" means to "pop back in place," and surely this is exactly what was happening as we hugged him and clung together, thanking the Lord for healing the fracture we had lived with for so long.

### Rebuilding a Relationship Takes Effort

After Larry returned, we began building our relationship completely anew, and we're still building it, learning more about each other all the time.

A lot of mail comes from parents who are trying to do the same thing. Once we get past the shock that comes when our children go off on a detour in life, one of our main concerns is how to relate to our son or daughter. We don't want to condone what they are doing, yet we don't want to condemn and judge either. After all, we are called to be witnesses, not judges.

Letters like the following are typical of people who are struggling to relate to their children:

> Our daughter, a junior at a Christian college, believes in the Lord and has a very caring heart, but has convinced herself that the Bible does not condemn her choice of lifestyle. We have told her that we love her and will always be here for her, but we do not agree with her on this issue. She seems to be getting in deeper and deeper and we need to know how to deal with all of this.

\* \* \* \* \* \*

> Mother's Day of this year, our 25-year-old son, whose background is in and out of drugs and alcohol, told us he thought he was gay. . . . Our hearts are broken and the first reaction was—"If you choose this life, you're no longer a member of this family." Since then, there have been conversations—pleading— and I'm sure you know the rest.

As I answer these letters, I try to share some of the principles I learned during the eleven years that Larry was estranged from us, as well as the years that have elapsed since he gave up his former lifestyle and became clean before God. The rest of this chapter will outline these principles and how to use them.

## 1. Stuff a Sock in Your Mouth

When the shock, anger, and rage first grip you, stuff a sock in your mouth and keep it there for at least six months. No matter how badly you want to lash out with Scripture verses, sermons, name-calling, or worse, just shut up. Venting your anger on your child will not help. I know. One thing that Larry told me after he returned was how my initial rage had hurt him. "Some of the things that you said were terrible," Larry told me. "They were like piercing swords."

The title of this chapter sums it up pretty well: Be careful of using words that cut and slash because there may come a day when you have to eat them. It reminds me of a little prayer I found in some of the "joy mail" a friend sent to me:

> Dear Father,
> help me to bridle my tongue,
> so that on judgment day
> I will not be found guilty
> of assault with a deadly weapon.

## 2. When the Going Gets Tough, Use Tough Love

When a child chooses a lifestyle that is self-destructive, he or she needs your love more than ever, but what's needed is *tough love*, not sloppy *agape* or syrupy sentimentality. I don't mean that parents should become mean or uncaring. Tough love is different and is usually the most difficult thing a parent can ever try to demonstrate. Whatever you do, you must learn not to let this loved one manipulate you. He may use lying, stealing, threats, flattery—you name it—to trap you into playing his game and thereby controlling you. Don't let that happen by keeping the following points in mind:

• You must not feel responsible for your child's addiction. This only makes you feel angry, depressed, guilty, and even physically ill.

• Do not try to rescue your loved one. Let your loved one hurt as a result of his or her own personal choices and actions. Parents should remember that they can't fur-line the pigpen for their prodigal kids.

• Accept the fact that this will be a very hard time for you, especially if you can observe daily the self-destructive addiction of your loved one. Try to treat yourself as lovingly and nurturingly as possible. Do things that are fun and enriching for you.

• Find a group that will give you support and the reassurance that it's necessary for you to become detached from the problem. Keep your compassion at a distance. You can't save this person, even if you want to.

• Your loved one is a very dependent person—not just on his or her particular vulnerable area, but on you. This person needs you more than you need him. He is a denier and will not face his dependency. You must face the truth, though, even if he won't; change your own life to get stronger and not let him pull you down.

• If your child threatens to leave without your ever seeing him or her again, remember that this is the rebellion lashing out at you. Actually, he needs you more than he'll ever admit. Your happiness does not really depend on him. You can survive, even if the threat is carried out. Even if you don't know where he is or how he is doing, you have given him to God and God has His hand on your child now. You can expect the adult child to continue to deny the truth as long as he is committed to staying out of fellowship. Remember that down deep he knows the truth, no matter what he says or how he rationalizes his behavior when he feels he's being "unjustly attacked."

• Tough love is tough on everybody! It hurts as much as surgery! But it's every bit as necessary. Stop telling yourself, *He's suffering so much. I must help him.* If you continue to "help" him, you will be helping him make wrong choices. Tough love is letting him hurt enough to get appropriate help.

• Remember that people don't seek help if they don't hurt. Tough love means letting go—completely. It means minding your own business. It means letting him have the dignity to pick up the pieces of his life and not be an emotional cripple any more. And do not worry that tough love will make you a calloused, unfeeling person. What it does do is give you an objectivity, much like that of a doctor who can perform needed surgery in order to save a life.

• Understand that he can't get well overnight. Long years of habit are hard to shake. If he tries to make you feel guilty, it's because he's frightened and angry. He may well have a way with words and can be quite charming, so be careful lest he manipulate you. Don't be fooled by his bluster and arrogance; he is only a paper tiger. You can learn how to live beyond his problems and not accept the consequences of his behavior as your own. Life is too short to be living in a practice hell. You have your right to get *his* monkey off *your* back. You can't let the sin of one person destroy the whole family.

• Selfishness, immaturity, and irresponsibility are all manifested in a rebellious spirit. He believes he is the important one. Nothing is as important as that which helps him get momentarily puffed up to serve his delusions of grandeur. The sooner you let go of his problem and let him take responsibility for it, himself, the better chance there will be that he will treat you with more respect.

• He feels sorry for himself, so when you learn to say no to his pleas for pity, he may see you as abandoning him. That's okay. He needs to take responsibility for his own choices. If he sees you worrying, it only rewards his attention-seeking. Rescuing someone keeps that person dependent on you and preserves a neurotic relationship. Being a rescuer may make you feel comfortable for a time, but the person you are rescuing may grow to resent you later.

• The kind of assurance the wayward one needs—that he's desirable and lovable—can come only from deep inside him. It will come only when he is willing to face his problem and do something about it.

• Have courage. If you act just one time out of self-respect instead of fear, you will feel better inside than you have probably felt in years. When you accept the reality of your loved one's vulnerable area, several things will happen. You will start getting rid of your personal anger toward him. You will begin to detach yourself from his manipulation, and you will start planning your life for you. Without your having to say it, he will see that the problem is his, not yours. You will have found your serenity and he will have a chance to choose recovery for himself.[4]

Beware of the blame game! It can cause the sin of one person to practically destroy the entire family. The mother blames herself, and sometimes the father blames the mother—or he

may decide to blame himself. Soon everyone is caught up in the "blame game," which is destructive to any family.

When Larry threatened to disown us (which he did) and change his name (which he also did), and then said he never wanted to see any of us again, all that was a dagger to my heart. But somehow I knew God would bring us through it. My mother's love for Larry never faltered, even as he drove that dagger deeper.

One thing that helped was that I had others who needed me. We had begun a ministry founded on Isaiah 61:1: "to bind up the brokenhearted. . . ." I couldn't let one child destroy my life, the rest of my family, and my faith in God. What Larry had done was a defeat, but it was only a TEMPORARY one. I had a choice. I could withdraw and become bitter or I could reach out to God with the knowledge that I would grow inwardly through all of this. I relied on 1 Kings 8:56 (KJV): "There hath not failed one word of all his good promise." I had God's promise that He loved me and He cared. As the psalmist says, "weeping may endure for a night, but joy cometh in the morning."[5]

As I put my trust in God, I began to realize my happiness really did not depend on what was happening in my son's life. God showed me that I could decorate my own life by helping others. The dawn does come. The sun does shine after the rain. There is peace after the storm. This poem came to mean a great deal:

> After a while you learn
> That love doesn't mean leaning,
> That kisses aren't contracts, and presents aren't promises . . .
> And you begin to accept defeats
> With your head up and your eyes open,
> With the grace of a woman, not the grief of a child.
> So you plant your own garden
> And decorate your own soul,
> Instead of waiting for someone to bring you flowers.
> And you learn that you can endure . . .
> That you really are strong
> And you really do have worth,
> And that with every new tomorrow
> Comes the dawn.
>
> Source unknown

Inside those long parentheses, while we waited with hope deferred, we prayed that God would do His work, according to His timetable, not ours, and that eventually Larry would make the choice to want to change his lifestyle. We knew we could not "fix" him or make any choices for him.

Now that Larry has been restored from his time of rebellion, God is using him in special ways. He works for the court system of Los Angeles and attends law school at night. Frequently, he talks with other young men who are struggling with their homosexual orientation and he is also a continual encouragement to me in Spatula Ministries. He is particularly helpful in doing research for my conference messages, as well as in preparation of the *Love Line* newsletter.

Larry is a real whiz with computers and he has access to all kinds of software. For example, if I need a Scripture verse, I just call Larry and he comes up with several that will fit. It is our goal to write a book together someday to share with other parents the principles of restoration through forgiveness and understanding that we have both learned through our years of estrangement.

So far in my list of guidelines, I've suggested that you "stuff a sock in your mouth" and use tough love to deal with your child's rebellion. Now I want to offer a third suggestion, one that applies to all parents and children:

### 3. Love Your Child Unconditionally

Not long after Larry left the gay lifestyle for good, we made a tape together that was sent out to the entire Spatula family. Some of that tape appears in *So, Stick a Geranium in Your Hat and Be Happy*,[6] but I want to share some additional parts of it here, which may be helpful to parents who are trying to build a better relationship with wayward children.

BARBARA: What would you suggest to young people who have gone off into a life of homosexuality and completely broken with their parents, saying they don't want anything to do with them? How can the parents show unconditional love to a child who is rebellious?

LARRY: There is a great need for people to understand the importance of committing their lives to being kind and loving. When a person does that, then they become righteous. They're doing what God wants, and as I've said, life is a web of relationships. When people respond properly, when they give out a loving attitude, others have to respond to that. If someone is very hateful, others respond to that as well.

BARBARA: We call it a "porcupine" type of love—when you love your kids and they shoot back those porcupine quills and say those awful things to you. Yet you have to love them unconditionally. It's our job to love and it's God's job to work in their lives. Kids may respond with a lot of retorts and unloving things, but if parents can still love them unconditionally, then I think God's going to honor that.

LARRY: God says that we are responsible for five things: words, thoughts, actions, deeds, and attitudes. In studying wisdom in the Scriptures and trying to understand the mind of God, I've come to realize that the words that come out of my mouth are only a reflection of the attitude I have within me. So, if I have a loving and a caring attitude, my words will reflect that.

BARBARA: Loving unconditionally is so important, but it's hard if your child doesn't communicate with you. All the years we didn't have any communication from you were difficult. It's very hard to show love when somebody doesn't respond. How do you think that worked in the years that you weren't in touch with us?

LARRY: I think that's when the parent has to turn it all over to God. Scripture says, "The king's heart is in the hand of the LORD, / Like the rivers of water; / He turns it wherever He wishes."[7] This verse tells me God turns people's hearts wherever He wants them to go. You've just got to trust God in those kinds of situations and know that God will touch their hearts at the right time.

I believe that what Larry was saying is that no one can love unconditionally in his or her own strength. You must trust God to turn the heart of your wayward child (and to keep your heart turned the right way, as well). Unconditional love is a beautiful ideal that is far beyond human strength. We must trust God for grace and patience, especially when the porcupine quills are flying thick and fast. And we must learn to FORGIVE. This is perhaps the most important building block of any loving relationship, and Larry and I talked about that as well.

## 4. Be Willing to Ask—and Receive—Forgiveness

As our interview continued, I asked Larry how he felt during all those years he was away.

BARBARA: Did you always feel that we loved you?
LARRY: I felt that there was a lot of animosity, but there was a lot of love, too; so I would say there was a lot of good and bad. But that was a time when we were both afraid of what was happening. We didn't know how to respond. It was a very difficult time for both of us. Fortunately, we have been able to put those things aside and to know the basic core relationship that a parent and a child can have.
BARBARA: So many parents have tried to train their kids to do the right thing, but they go off and do their own thing. And so the parents feel guilt because they believe they have failed. It's hard to explain to parents that they are not responsible for their kids' choices.
LARRY: I think that when parents have a problem with a child, it's time for the parents to examine their hearts and minds. God is using those problems to highlight certain principles that have been neglected, and if parents neglect those principles then the whole family suffers for it.
BARBARA: I think one thing we're going to have to learn to do as parents is to zip up the past because we've all made mistakes. We have to say, "The past is over, yesterday is a canceled check, tomorrow is a promissory note, but today is cash. Today I haven't made any mistakes—yet. You can start out every day fresh and new to serve the Lord and how wonderful it is to start out every day and know the past is over. You don't have to live in bondage to things that were in the past that were unhappy for you, and I don't have to, either.

LARRY: That's because we've been able to forgive each other. Forgiveness is a very powerful thing—not only the ability to forgive, but the ability to be forgiven. When someone comes to you and says, "I was wrong in what I did to you; will you forgive me?" that's a very powerful thing because it releases a burden of guilt we carry because of whoever we have offended. But what holds people back from doing that is their own pride, their own inability to say, "I made a mistake, I was wrong." A lot of parents don't want to do that, and when the child sees the parent not willing to admit his mistakes, what makes you think the child would want to admit any mistakes?

BARBARA: In many cases parents need to ask their children to forgive them for their lack of love, but a lot of parents say, "Why should I ask forgiveness? What did I do? My kids went off into the gay life. I didn't do anything." But it's that attitude that's wrong and it won't help any kind of relationship. Parents should ask their child for forgiveness when they haven't shown understanding or love. That's the beginning of spiritual growth. Parents have to grow and change through all this as well as their children.

LARRY: Another important fact is that when a person is reacting so violently or so angrily, it's time for the other person the parent—to examine his or her life to see what it is that brought this on. Is it an attitude of pride or an unbroken spirit? The parents should not look on themselves as authoritarians, but rather as friends of their grown children. And if they've offended them, the parents should go to the children and ask for their forgiveness. You'll find a lot of parents aren't willing to do that.

BARBARA: There's no perfect parent. After all, God had problems with Adam. We try to be perfect parents, but we're not and we fail.

LARRY: Everyone fails, but that's why Christ came. That's why we have the Bible and those principles to live by. We need to realize that we can admit our failures and be able to put them aside.

One of the key words Larry used in our interview is *friend*. Parents will move a long way toward building a better relationship with their adult children when they realize they must become more the friend and less the parental "authority." The following words by William Arthur Ward describe the kind of friends we want to be to our kids:

A FRIEND IS . . .

A friend is one who is not hard to find when you are penniless.

A friend is one who makes your grief less painful, your adversity more bearable.

A friend is one who joyfully sings with you when you are on the mountaintop, and silently walks beside you through the valley.

A friend is one with whom you are comfortable, to whom you are loyal, through whom you are blessed, and for whom you are grateful.

A friend is one who warms you by his presence, trusts you with his secrets, and remembers you in his prayers.

A friend is one who gives you a spark of assurance when you doubt your ability to fulfill your noblest aspiration, climb your special mountain, or reach your secret goal.

A friend is one who helps you bridge the gaps between loneliness and fellowship, frustration and confidence, despair and hope, setbacks and success.

A friend is one who is available to you, understanding of you, and patient with you. A friend is no less a gift from God than is a talent; no less a treasure than life itself.

A friend is also someone who listens.

## 5. Listen More, Talk a Lot Less

The last line of the essay quoted above mentions listening, one of the most powerful tools available for building good relationships with friends and loved ones. There is a lot of talk about "communication" today, and it's true that we all need to learn how to communicate better with each other. But communication can become just another buzz word that doesn't mean much. On the other hand, listening is something specific that any of us can do if we want to try. Most people think communicating means doing a lot of talking, but, in truth, I think real communication begins when you start listening to the other person. As James says, be QUICK to listen and SLOW to speak.[8] A good definition of listening is this:

ATTENTION WITH THE INTENTION
TO UNDERSTAND THE OTHER PERSON.[9]

In his excellent book on communication, *Speaking from the Heart*, Ken Durham writes:

Christian listening is an act which communicates to another, "Right now, I am here for you. No one else, just you. I want to hear and understand what you have to say. I'm all yours." Listening is allowing the other person to set the agenda for the conversation, seeking to clarify his point of view. Ultimately, listening is helping a person to understand himself better.[10]

The following poem sums up Christian listening very well:

LISTEN

When I ask you to listen to me
and you start giving advice
you have not done what I asked.

When I ask you to listen to me
and you begin to tell me why I shouldn't feel that way
you are trampling on my feelings.

When I ask you to listen to me
and you feel you have to do something to solve my problem
you have failed me, strange as that may seem.

So please listen and just hear me.
And, if you want to talk,

wait a minute for your turn;
and I'll listen to you.

Source unknown

If you are having trouble communicating with your son or daughter . . . if you simply "can't talk about it" . . . maybe the best thing you can do is to invite your loved one to share feelings. Put away your desire to quote Scripture, give advice, or lecture. Two of my favorite mottoes are:

NOBODY CARES HOW MUCH YOU KNOW
UNLESS THEY KNOW HOW MUCH YOU CARE.

\*   \*   \*   \*   \*   \*

TALKING IS SHARING . . .
LISTENING IS CARING.

A lasting gift to a child, including grown children, is the gift of a parent's listening ear—and heart. Listen first and talk afterward. Then, instead of saying things that may bruise and cut, your words will be pleasant, like honey, sweet to the soul of your child[11] and healing to your relationship.

**Splish/Splash . . .**

SOME PEOPLE FIND FAULT
LIKE THERE WAS A REWARD FOR IT.

\*   \*   \*   \*   \*   \*

TAKE A TIP FROM NATURE . . .
YOUR EARS AREN'T MADE TO SHUT,
BUT YOUR MOUTH IS.

\*   \*   \*   \*   \*   \*

OPPORTUNITIES ARE OFTEN MISSED
BECAUSE WE ARE BROADCASTING
WHEN WE SHOULD BE LISTENING.

\* \* \* \* \* \*

NEVER WASTE YOUR PAIN!

Dear Lord . . .
Please grant that I shall
Never waste my pain; for . . .
To fail without learning,
To fall without getting up,
To sin without overcoming,
To be hurt without forgiving,
To be discontent without improving,
To be crushed without becoming more caring,
To suffer without growing more sensitive,
Makes of suffering a senseless, futile exercise,
A tragic loss,
And of pain,
The greatest waste of all.

Dick Innes

\* \* \* \* \* \*

THE ONLY CONDITION FOR LOVING
IS TO LOVE WITHOUT CONDITIONS.

\* \* \* \* \* \*

Self-control means controlling the tongue! A quick retort can ruin everything. (Prov. 13:3, TLB)

## We Are Easter People
## Living in a Good Friday World

*Due to the shortage of trained trumpeters,*
*the end of the world will be postponed three months.*

Folks often ask me, "Barb, where do you get your joy?" That question always makes me think of the thirteenth verse of 1 Corinthians 13, the "love chapter": "And now these three remain: Faith, hope and love. But the greatest of these is love" (NIV).

With so many cesspools to fall into in life, we need a spring we can go to for splashes of joy—a spring full of living water that only Jesus provides.

### Joy Begins with Faith

I love the line Tony Campolo uses—surely one of the greatest statements of faith ever written: "It's Friday, but Sunday's Comin'."

On that first Good Friday, Jesus' followers were in a real cesspool. Jesus had been nailed to a cross and now He was dead. Mary was distraught with grief. The disciples were scattered like frightened sheep. Pilate was confident he had washed his hands of the whole mess. Unbelievers were cynically saying that this so-called Messiah hadn't changed a thing. And worst of all, Satan was dancing around saying, "I won! I won!"

Yes, it was Friday, but then the temple veil split open like an overripe watermelon, rocks moved, tombs opened up, and the Roman centurion who had been sent to oversee the execution of some troublemaker wound up babbling, "This WAS the Son of God!"

And then came Sunday. Mary Magdalene and the other women came to Jesus' sealed and guarded tomb to find the stone rolled away and an angel in blazing white saying, "He is not here—He is risen!"

On Friday all had been darkness, despair, and grief. But NOW it was SUNDAY and the whole world had cause for joy greater than any known before or since.

Actually, we aren't Easter people living in a Good Friday world, we are RESURRECTION people.

As an unknown writer said:

> Resurrection says that absolutely nothing can separate me from the love of God. Not sin or my stupidity. Not the sinister or the selfish, not the senseless or the secular.

The foundation of all joy for Christians is that we can live as though Christ died yesterday, rose today, and is coming tomorrow. It starts here and it's for everyone, no strings, no admission fee, because we are saved by grace and grace alone. That's what Paul meant when he said we are saved by grace through faith (Eph. 2:8, 9). It doesn't have anything to do with what we can do. As I always say,

JUSTICE IS WHEN WE GET WHAT WE DESERVE.
MERCY IS WHEN WE DON'T GET WHAT WE DESERVE.
BUT GRACE IS WHEN WE GET WHAT WE DON'T DESERVE.

Grace is God's unmerited favor which is showered upon us. And that grace is FREE to all who ask for it. We begin by trusting Jesus Christ. That's it. He is our first experience of joy. And we continue to have splashes of joy as we learn to trust in Him alone.

But what about the times we slide back into that cesspool of despair? Has God forsaken us? We have questions and more questions. WHY? HOW? WHERE ARE YOU, LORD? As Ruth Harms Calkins writes:

> Lord, I ask more questions
> Than You ask.
> The ratio, I would suppose
> Is ten to one.
>
> I ask:
> Why do You permit this anguish?
> How long can I endure it?
> What possible purpose does it serve?
> Have You forgotten to be gracious?
> Have I wearied You?
> Have I offended You?
> Have You cast me off?
> Where did I miss Your guidance?
> When did I lose the way?
> Do You see my utter despair?
>
> You ask:
> *Are you trusting me?*[1]

Ruth Calkins's words remind me that there are 354 "fear nots" in the Bible—almost one for each day of the year. If we feed our faith, our doubts will starve to death. The feeblest knock of faith opens heaven's door because faith looks beyond the darkness of earth to the brightness of heaven.

Before he died, I heard my good friend Walter Martin tell about the time he and two agnostics were guests on the "Phil Donahue Show." Topics for the day included death, heaven, and the penalty for sin. As the program drew to a close, Phil Donahue went up to Dr. Martin in his familiar way and said, "Well, now, Doc, don't you think that when I get to the end of the road, God will put His arms around me and say, 'Aw, c'mon in, Phil!'?"

Dr. Martin flashed Phil Donahue a wide smile and responded, "Oh, Phil, He already did—two thousand years ago. He invited you to come on in THEN."

When I think about this story, it brings tears to my eyes as I realize how God made it possible for us to be assured of heaven because of His loving sacrifice for us. We have an open invitation with a heavenly R.S.V.P.

Walter Martin is now with the Lord, but his response to Phil Donahue that day is a splash of joy that still continues to encourage me. It gives me extra courage when I need it. It is so true: Our WORDS OF FAITH go on long after we are gone.

## Joy Comes Out of Hope

One of the cleverest—and saddest—epitaphs I ever heard appears on the headstone of Mel Blanc, voice of so many famous cartoon characters, including Porky Pig and Elmer Fudd:

TH-TH-TH-THAT'S ALL, FOLKS!

I don't know what Mel Blanc personally believed about life after death, but this life ISN'T all, folks. There is, oh, so much more! We don't face a hopeless end because we have an endless hope! Our hope is in the FACT that, because of our faith, we are going UP. Somebody sent me these thoughts on the word UP, adapted from an essay by Frank Endicott:

WHAT'S UP?

We have a two-letter word we use constantly that may have more meanings than you would imagine. The word is UP.

It is easy to understand UP meaning toward the sky or toward the top of a list. But when we waken, why do we wake UP? At a meeting, why does a topic come UP, why do participants speak UP, and why are the officers UP for election? And why is it UP to the secretary to write UP a report?

Often the little word isn't needed, but we use it anyway. We brighten UP a room, polish UP the silver, lock UP the house, and fix UP the old car. At other times, it has special meanings. People stir UP trouble, line UP for tickets, work UP an appetite, think UP excuses, get tied UP in traffic. To be dressed is one thing, but to be dressed UP is special. It may be confusing, but a drain must be opened UP because it is stopped UP. We open UP a store in the morning and close it UP at night. We seem to be mixed UP about UP.

To be UP on the proper use of UP, look UP the word in your dictionary. In one desk-size dictionary UP takes UP half a page, and listed definitions add UP to about 40. If you are UP to it, you might try building UP a list of the many ways in which UP is used. It will take UP a lot of your time but, if you don't give UP, you may wind UP with a thousand.

Frank Endicott cleverly lists a lot of uses for the word UP, but he forgot two important ones. First, there are a lot of people who need to CHEER UP, and, second, one way or another, Christians are going UP—to heaven—to eternal life with Jesus. I like the picture of going UP in Psalm 90:10 (RSV) which says: "The years of our life are threescore and ten, or even by reason of strength, fourscore; yet their span is but toil and trouble; they are soon gone, and we fly away."

Can you believe it says we will FLY AWAY? I can't be sure that the psalmist was thinking of the Second Coming when he wrote those lines, but he pictures exactly what Paul says in 1 Thessalonians 4:16, 17 (NKJV):

> For the Lord Himself will descend from heaven with a shout, with the voice of an archangel, and with the trumpet of God. And the dead in Christ will rise first. Then we who are alive and remain shall be caught up together with them in the clouds to meet the Lord in the air. And thus we shall always be with the Lord.

That blessed hope of the Christian is all wrapped UP in the Second Coming. I often urge folks to get in plenty of "rapture practice" by going out in the backyard and jumping UP and down, just to limber UP for the big day when the trumpet sounds and we all go UP. As I like to say,

HE'S GONNA TOOT
AND WE'RE GONNA SCOOT!

I often mention rapture practice when I speak, and once an elderly lady came up afterward and asked, "Honey, when you do your rapture practice, do you do it on a trampoline or on the grass?"

I also love the letter from the lady who said she and her husband were planning to celebrate their fiftieth wedding anniversary by going up in a hot-air balloon. She said, "I'm going to stick a geranium in my hat and be happy and have a terrific pre-rapture joy ride!"

Sometimes I talk with folks who wonder WHEN Jesus is coming. Down through the years different people have "set the date," but they have forgotten one thing: The Bible never sets the date. Meanwhile, it's a Good Friday world, full of pain, guilt, and shame. AIDS stalks the earth, killing thousands, and it will take thousands more before a cure is found—if ever. I have found a plaque that I often give to AIDS victims to remind them and their families of the endless hope all believers have beyond this life. The picture shows Jesus taking someone into His arms and hugging him, and the words say:

WHEN I COME HOME TO HEAVEN

When I come home to Heaven
    How joyful it will be!
For on that day at last
    My risen Lord I'll see.

No greater happiness than
    To see Him face to face,

> To see the love in His eyes
>   And feel His warm embrace.
>
> I've done nothing to deserve
>   That perfect home above.
> It was given freely through
>   The grace of Jesus' love.
>
> Then why should earthly cares
>   Weigh down upon me so?
> They'll be a distant memory
>   When home at last I go.[2]

As I said in chapter 3, hope is hard to kill. In fact, it has saved the life of more than one person who felt hopeless. A note that came in the mail, and which I treasure very much, says:

> Thank you for your book . . . God really spoke to me through your words. I'm a sophomore medical student. Stress, anxiety and depression were my constant companions . . . suicide was never too far from my door. Now I have hope . . . Thank you.

Somebody said one of our greatest enemies is not disease—it's despair. One of our greatest friends is hope. And the reason we can have hope in this life is because of our hope in the life to come. I have always liked acrostics, and this one says it all about hope:

> He
> Offers
> Peace
> Eternal.

## But the Greatest Joy Is Love

One of the happiest phrases in all of Scripture is tucked away in 1 John 4:8: "GOD IS LOVE." And I like to add, "GOD IS JOY." To know and feel God's love is to know the deep kind of abiding joy that you want to splash all over others.

Jesus reassured us that He would not leave us comfortless (see John 14:18). He did not promise endless days of ease, but rather love and growth as we travel over the bumps and wash-outs in life. He didn't say we would all ride in limos. We might make our trip in a beat-up station wagon, a pickup truck, on a bicycle, or even in a wheelchair. No matter how we travel, the important thing is feeling God's breath upon us. We need a quickening that lets us know God IS love and we can have fellowship with Him.

Sometimes it helps to get away alone in a lovely setting. It could be at the ocean with the waves crashing on the beach, or it might be while bobbing around in a sailboat, or just walking along a path and feeling the breeze blowing through the trees.

But God's love can happen ANYWHERE. Once it happened to me at the Department of Motor Vehicles office when I was selecting a personalized license plate for Bill. As I looked through the giant book of license-plate names that had already been used, I realized that my own name is written in another book that is much more important—the Lamb's Book of Life, and that I am forever a daughter of the King. God reminded me that I am His child. I am royalty! God's warm comfort blanket enfolded me with the assurance of His care. I felt His presence so strongly that I had tears in my eyes. The warm comforting feeling of His love splashed over me—EVEN AT THE DMV!

But the specific place really doesn't matter. Being marinated in God's love is what counts. It's your personal relationship with God that makes the difference and brings the joy from His fountain of life. Experience has taught me that only those who have gone from despair to hope can know what a refreshing fountain of life feels like. One of my favorite thoughts is:

GOD LOVES A DANGLING CHRISTIAN.

In other words, God wants the believer to be TOTALLY dependent on Him. And when you cry out to Him for help, His

love is the rope that pulls you out of the cesspool to His refreshing fountain. Once you come to the fountain and have
been splashed with God's joy, something happens. You realize that you aren't the only one who knows what a cesspool is
like. Sometimes in our loneliness it is easy to think we are the
only ones who have had to suffer, "just like this." But when
God's love touches us during our suffering, we can see how
shallow our caring for others has been.

C. S. Lewis has said that grief is like a long, winding valley,
where any bend might reveal a totally new landscape. And
when we come upon that beautiful new landscape, we have a
clear vision of what it means to be a spirit lifter. Love is the
greatest gift we have to give, and if we let Him, God will help
us be sensitive to loneliness, grief, and pain wherever it ex-
ists—which is all around us.

## God Always Needs More Pipe

Think of a gardener irrigating his garden. He is able to channel life-giving water to all areas except to one little dying plant
way over in the corner. The gardener knows that if he had just
one more piece of pipe he could run it over to that wilting plant
and transform it with new life.

So it is with the Master Gardener. Because He chooses to
minister through us, He needs many lengths of pipe to bless
persons here, there, and all around. Perhaps in your area there
is a drooping, wilting person who needs God's touch right now.
Proverbs says, "Anxious hearts are very heavy, but a word of
encouragement does wonders."[3]

We can be that extra piece of pipe through which He can
channel His cheer, encouragement, and joy to those who need
it. Christ, Himself, set the example of what it means to be a
spirit-lifter. On the night before He died, during one of the dark-
est moments that He and His disciples had ever known in the
three years that they had been together, He told them to "cheer
up, for I have overcome the world."[4]

At Spatula Ministries we feel our usual way of being a pipeline is through answering letters and making phone calls,
sometimes to very frantic, despairing people on the other end
of the line. We also go out to speak all over the country, and
once a month we conduct a support group for parents of gay
children, which is a prototype for dozens of such groups all
over the nation. But sometimes God asks us to run a very personal pipeline directly to someone who needs a special bit of
TLC.

### Greg's Mom Received His Suicide Tape

About 11:00 on a Saturday morning last year I got a frantic
call from a mother who said, "My son, Greg, lives in La Habra
and he just sent me a tape cassette saying he is HIV positive
and is going to take his life. Would you go find him? We don't
know who else to call."

As I talked with this mother, I learned that she and her husband had been on a trip and had gotten back to their home in
Idaho sooner than expected. When they arrived back home,
the tape was waiting, and she was sure her son had thought
that by the time they were supposed to hear the tape several
days later, he would have already taken his life.

Greg's mother gave me his address, and I left immediately
to try to find him. His apartment was only about three miles
from my home and I drove as fast as I could, thinking of the
days that had elapsed since he had sent his mother the tape.
What if it were too late?

I pulled up to an old apartment complex where this young
man was supposed to be and discovered it had just been
painted. The Spanish architecture was now garish shades of
orchid and turquoise, and there were no numbers on any of
the apartments because the painters had taken them down temporarily.

I went from door to door, asking everyone about a young
man named Greg, but nobody there seemed to speak English

and my Spanish is pretty much forgotten so I got no positive responses. I was beginning to think I had the wrong address when, on my way toward the front of the building, I saw one door ajar. Thinking perhaps it was the laundry room, I pushed it all the way open and looked inside. The tiny room was dark and dank, and smelled like cat dung. The only furniture was a long, skinny bed, a table, and a chair. Then, in the semi-darkness, I made out a tall, dark, emaciated young man who just sat there, staring into space.

"Are you Greg?" I asked.

Startled, the young man looked up at me and said, "Yes, but who are you?"

I told him who I was and that his mother had called me that morning and had wanted me to see him. "God really loves you, Greg," I said. "Whatever you've been into, God loves you and He'll forgive you. God won't turn His back on you. You may have strayed off, but I want you to know that Jesus died for your sins and still loves you and wants to welcome you back. Can I pray with you? Can I talk with you?"

I prayed with Greg and then we talked for almost an hour. He told me he couldn't believe anybody would care that much for him. He'd gone to a Christian college for awhile, and when students there learned that he was gay he would find notes taped on his door that said, "GET OUT, YOU FAGGOT!"

Finally he had left college and dropped totally into the gay lifestyle. But mental conviction hounded him because he knew it was wrong. He left Long Beach and moved to La Habra to make a fresh start and forsake all the sinful past. But just after taking his first step to restoration with God, he learned he had a full-blown case of AIDS.

Greg also told me that he had no money, hadn't eaten for days, and his car was about to be repossessed. He had planned to kill himself that very day by using sleeping pills, and to prove it, he held up a bottle full of them.

I reached into my purse and gave him all the cash I had with me—thirty-five dollars. Then I said, "Greg, I'm going out to get you some food and other stuff. Please don't do anything desperate while I'm gone. I'll be back soon."

Greg promised that he would wait for me, and I went home and told Bill the story. While Bill scraped up some money, I went out to the supermarket and bought some eggs, cheese, bread, and other groceries, as well as some vitamins. Then I hurried back to Greg's apartment. I had only been gone for an hour, but when I got there it was locked and there was no response to my knock on the door.

I found the apartment manager and said, "I need to get into this young man's apartment because I was here an hour ago and I need to put away some groceries."

"I don't know what's going on with him," the lady said. "He's lived here a week, but he's never been out of the apartment. Nobody ever comes to see him, and I saw his car being towed away about an hour ago."

The woman let me in, and when I opened Greg's refrigerator there was nothing in it but half a can of 7-Up. I put away the groceries. I left a note with my phone number that said, "Greg, I don't know where you are, but please call me as soon as you get back."

When I got home the phone was ringing and it was Greg! "I just can't believe that anybody would do this," he told me. "I'd gone out to get some groceries with the thirty-five dollars because I hadn't eaten anything all week. I just can't believe that God would really care about me."

The next day I took Greg up to a church in the Glendora area and got him involved in a support group for AIDS victims. They took him under their wing and worked out transportation so he could get up to the church for support-group meetings and Sunday services.

It turned out that Greg has a beautiful voice and he soon had a tremendous ministry at the church, singing for all kinds of events, including funerals of young men in his support group who died from AIDS.

Meanwhile, Greg continued living at the orchid and turquoise apartment house and went back to a job he had in an office two miles away. With his car repossessed, Greg faced walking that distance each day, but, fortunately, some friends provided him with a bike. For the next several months he used that to go back and forth to work. The route to Greg's office went right by our house and he would often stop by for a snack or just to visit on his way home. It was hot and smoggy, but Greg never complained. He considered himself fortunate to be able to ride the bike to work and back.

Just before Christmas Greg was transferred to a branch office about thirty miles from La Habra. The good news was that it was much closer to the church where he loved to be with new Christian friends after making a complete break with the old gay lifestyle. The bad news was that he had to move to a new place that was farther away from his job, and he was in desperate need of a car.

By this time we had really learned to love Greg and we were concerned about how he would manage with moving and getting back and forth to work. One day Bill came in and told me he had just had a revelation. Because Bill has very few revelations, I was all ears.

"I'm going to give Wumphee to Greg so that he can get moved and keep his job!" Bill said.

Earlier, I said that my nickname for Bill is "Wumphee." I also mentioned that I had gotten him personalized license plates for his 1974 Oldsmobile, a car that should have been a tuna boat—at least it's as big as one. Wumphee seemed to me to be the obvious choice for the license plates, so that's how his beloved car came to be nicknamed Wumphee, too. The only problem was that as soon as he bolted on the personalized plates, service-station attendants everywhere started calling Bill "Mr. Wumphee." He said it was bad enough having his wife call him that, but having to hear, "Have a nice day, Mr. Wumphee" every time he filled up was almost too much.

Despite all that, Bill loved Wumphee, so I knew that giving the car to Greg was no small gesture on his part. Not only that, but Bill cleaned out the car, filled Wumphee's giant tank with gas, and also put a case of oil in the trunk (Wumphee burns almost as much oil as gas).

All of this really surprised me because Bill is known for his Swedish frugality (i.e., being tight). As a final touch, we put a lot of nickels, dimes, and quarters in the ashtray so passengers would be encouraged not to smoke in the car, and Greg would have plenty of change for parking meters—or hamburgers.

The next time Greg came by, Bill handed him the car title for Wumphee. Not much for ceremony or sentimentality, all he said was, "Everything works. You don't need to do anything to Wumphee, just keep oil in him because he does burn a lot of oil."

We all celebrated on that joyful day. Bill got a splash of joy when he saw Greg's eyes light up over the car, and I felt so relieved that Greg's transportation problem was solved, and so simply! Just before Greg drove off tooting the horn, Bill mentioned that when Greg got his own license plates, he wanted back the personalized plates. Greg was more than happy to return them and now the WUMPHEE plates are proudly displayed in our joy room.

## Greg Knows That God Is Real

Since that day when Greg's mother made her frantic phone call, she and her husband have kept in touch with him. They came down to help him get moved and while here they also attended a Spatula meeting and became strong supporters of the ministry. As I completed this chapter, Greg was coping with his illness and had the energy to work and minister with his musical ability in many different settings.

Not long after I found Greg on the verge of suicide, I contacted Marilyn Meberg, one of the teachers he had had at college. He remembered her fondly as someone who was a "bright spot" in his life at that time. I told Marilyn Greg's story and she was thrilled, because she was in the midst of preparing some new presentations on God's love and care—the way He is a shepherd to all of His sheep. She wrote to him, and she and Greg have agreed to share parts of their letters with you:

Greg,

My heart breaks for the pain you've experienced from the isolation and support you did not receive, and more than anything, the fear that God, too, had turned His back on you. How unlike the nature of God to abandon us and yet, how prone we are to think He probably feels toward us like others do. It knocks my socks off that God should direct Barb to your door on the very day when you most needed Him. I stumbled across an incredible couple of verses that fit your experience. Ezekiel 34:11, 12 says: "Behold, I Myself will search for My sheep and seek them out. As a shepherd cares for his herd in the day when he is among his scattered sheep, so I will care for My sheep and will deliver them from all the places to which they were scattered on a cloudy and gloomy day."

Dear, dear Greg—God has searched you out, found you among the "scattered" and draws you to Himself that you might know you are esteemed and loved! Unfortunately, all too often the "sheep" do not have the compassion and acceptance of the Shepherd. We hurt each other inexcusably. Don't confuse their actions with those of the Shepherd. There are no conditions from Him, Greg—only believe in Him and receive Him. WHAT A DEAL! God love you, Greg, and hold you close!

Marilyn Meberg

Not long afterward, Marilyn received this letter from Greg:

Dear Mrs. Meberg,

Thank you for sharing Ezekiel 34. As I sit here just blown over by the blessings that God has bestowed on this little wandering sheep, I'm overwhelmed. He has indeed searched for me out of the places I've wandered, not just physical places but those places in my heart that have wandered away from His warmth and slowly gotten cold. I want to say a couple of things. For the first time in my life I know that God is real. No more looking at the menu and admiring the nice pictures of the food; my meal has come and I've tasted its fullness. I know that death is real, I've seen it in the eyes of my friend, Brent, and I know that one day I, too, am going too die. And I know that the Shepherd who gathered me unto Himself here will welcome me when I get on the other side.

For Christmas, Greg gave me a darling Erma Bombeck calendar and each day, as I tear off a sheet, I think of him and his wonderful sense of humor and the talents he is using so effectively for the Lord. On one occasion I gave him an assignment to look up a great many Scriptures for me to include in something I was doing for the *Love Line* newsletter. He diligently finished the task and brought the list to me. It represented hours of work, and Greg was so proud that he had accomplished all that I had asked of him because he wanted, in some way, to do something for us after what we had done for him. That is how the principle works:

> AS WE REFRESH OTHERS,
> WE, OURSELVES, ARE REFRESHED.

### Take Time to Love

In sharing Greg's story, we see so many who are hurting because they are in one cesspool or another. If you have been touched with God's love, He wants you to take time to touch others. As the final line of a well-known poem puts it:

> TAKE TIME TO LOVE—IT'S GOD-LIKE.

There is no limit to the lives you might touch for the Master if you decide to become a pipeline for His love. You have probably read the following poem somewhere, sometime. It is very well known and it has been repeated in one form or another in many places. "The Old Violin" is included here because it states so clearly the message of this chapter:

'Twas battered and scarred, and the auctioneer
Thought it scarcely worth his while
To waste much time on the old violin,
But held it up with a smile.
"What am I bidden, good folks?" he cried.
"Who'll start the bidding for me?
A dollar, a dollar—now two, only two—
Two dollars, and who'll make it three?
Three dollars once, three dollars twice,
Going for three"—but no!
From the room far back a grey-haired man
Came forward and picked up the bow;
Then wiping the dust from the old violin,
And tightening up all the strings,
He played a melody pure and sweet;
As sweet as an angel sings.
The music ceased, and the auctioneer,
With a voice that was quiet and low,
Said, "What am I bid for the old violin?"
And he held it up with the bow.
"A thousand dollars—and who'll make it two?
Two thousand—and who'll make it three?
Three thousand once and three thousand twice—
And going and gone!" said he.
The people cheered but some of them cried,
"We do not quite understand—
What changed its worth?" The man replied:
"The touch of the master's hand!"

And many a man with life out of tune,
And battered and torn with sin,
Is auctioned cheap to a thoughtless crowd,
Much like the old violin . . .
But the Master comes, and the foolish crowd
Never can quite understand
The worth of a soul and the change that's wrought
By the Touch of the Master's Hand.
                                    Myra Brooks Welch[5]

There are many ways to touch people for the Master. In other books, I've shared about wrapping a brick with gold-foil paper and giving it to folks as a gift.[6] It serves as a perfect doorstop and it's inexpensive and easy to make. I suggest that first you make one of these bricks for yourself. Get a used brick or buy a new one for a few cents at a builder's supply store. Find some bright shiny GOLD wrapping paper and wrap the brick carefully. Then put on a colorful bow and perhaps some cherries or berries or some other sprig of color.

Now you have a beautiful reminder that you are GOLD IN THE MAKING! The furnace of pain you have come through or are going through has made you as gold for the Master's use! You have been and are being refined, purified, tried—being made WORTHY!

Do you know, if all the gold in the whole world were melted down into a solid cube it would be about the size of an eight-room house? If you got possession of all that gold—billions of dollars' worth—you could not buy a friend, character, peace of mind, a clear conscience, or eternal life. Yet you are GOLD IN THE MAKING because of the trials you have come through. Now, THAT'S an exciting idea!

After you have your own shiny gold brick, nicely sitting by your door as a stopper, make another such brick for a good friend. Perhaps it is someone who has been a "gold brick" in your life and has refreshed and encouraged you, and they may be needing a lift of their own right now. Take your gift to this friend and tell her how she has refreshed and encouraged you. Tell her you want to thank her for how she has helped you through your own time of testing and that you want to remind her that she, too, is gold in the making.

Before long, you may be making many other gold bricks to share with other friends who are like gold in your life.

Something else I've been doing lately is wrapping up a small piece of wood about the size of a match box. I use bright, shiny paper, complete with ribbon, and send it to friends with the following message taped on the box:

> This is a special gift
> That you can never see
> The reason it's so special is
> It's just for you . . . from me.
> Whenever you are happy,
> Or even feeling blue,
> You only have to see this gift
> And know I think of you.
> You never can unwrap it,
> Please leave the ribbon tied . . .
> Just hold it close to your heart
> It's filled with LOVE inside.

Those are just a couple of ideas—nothing profound or expensive—but simple ways to reach out to touch someone for the Master and spread some splashes of joy in a cesspool world. You may prefer another approach, but the important thing is to do SOMETHING. As one lady's letter put it:

> PRETEND YOU'RE A STAR
> AND POKE A HOLE IN SOMEONE'S DARKNESS.

## Larry Sends a Serendipity

As I was closing an interview with Dr. James Dobson on his "Focus on the Family" broadcast, he had some nice things to say about Spatula Ministries:

> Barbara, it's quite an act of compassion that you allow people that you don't even know to reach out to you with such misery. Most of us have such difficulties in our own lives we don't need anybody else's. And it's one thing to put your arm around a brother or sister at church who is hurting, someone that you've known through the years and try to help them; it's another thing to try to tell the whole world that you'll accept their problems—not only their problems, but their misery. You have done that through the years. I don't know many people like that. My hat is off to you. It doesn't have a geranium in it, but it's off to you. I really do appreciate who you are.

Slightly embarrassed, I was trying to tell Dr. Dobson I appreciated his kind words and his ready smile, but he interrupted me saying he had a surprise that would put a smile on MY face. "We have placed a phone call just a short time ago to Barbara's son—the one she has referred to a number of times," he told the radio audience. "He has a message that we want to leave with all of you."

Then I heard Larry's voice saying these unforgettable words:

The eleven years of estrangement were difficult years for both my parents and me. And during that time it became very evident to me of the gripping power of bitterness and resentment that had engulfed our family. But now, however, we're all grateful for God's healing restoration.

And if you've read my mother's book, *So, Stick a Geranium in Your Hat and Be Happy,* you'll know the details and the impact of her ministry on my situation and on those people who have been similarly situated. I'm thankful for you and all your listeners who have prayed for me and my family and can only offer this word of advice at this time:

If we as Christians can purpose in our hearts to be kind and loving in all that we do and put away a condemning spirit and learn the fear of the Lord, then surely the light of Christ will be able to shine in our disbelieving world, and restoration and revival will take root in the lives of those that we touch on a daily basis.

To sit there and hear my darling son say those words after the long years of estrangement wasn't a mere splash of joy, IT WAS LIKE A TIDAL WAVE! As his mom, and more importantly now, AS HIS BEST FRIEND, all I can say is . . .

WHOOPEE!

**Splish/Splash . . .**

HAPPINESS IS LIKE JAM:
YOU CAN'T SPREAD IT WITHOUT

GETTING SOME ON YOURSELF.

\* \* \* \* \* \*

WHEN GOD MEASURES A PERSON,
HE PUTS A TAPE AROUND THE HEART
INSTEAD OF THE HEAD.

\* \* \* \* \* \*

HE LOVES EACH OF US,
AS IF THERE WERE ONLY ONE OF US.
St. Augustine

\* \* \* \* \* \*

LOVE . . .

is the one treasure that multiplies by division: It is the one gift
that grows bigger the more you take from it. It is the one business in which it pays to be an absolute spendthrift; give it away,
throw it away, splash it over, empty your pockets, shake the
basket, turn the glass upside down, and tomorrow you will have
more than ever.

Source unknown

\* \* \* \* \* \*

SALVATION
DON'T LEAVE EARTH WITHOUT IT!

\* \* \* \* \* \*

GIVE LAVISHLY! LIVE ABUNDANTLY!

The more you give, the more you get—
The more you laugh, the less you fret—
The more you do unselfishly,

The more you live abundantly . . .
The more of everything you share,
The more you'll always have to spare—
The more you love, the more you'll find
That life is good and friends are kind . . .
For only what we give away
Enriches us from day to day.

                              Source unknown


            *    *    *    *    *    *


THINGS BEYOND OUR SEEING
THINGS BEYOND OUR HEARING
THINGS BEYOND OUR IMAGINING
ALL PREPARED BY GOD
FOR THOSE WHO LOVE HIM.


            *    *    *    *    *    *


And you can also be very sure that God will rescue the children of the godly. (Prov. 11:21, TLB)

## *Going Up with a Splash*

*Life is too short to eat brown bananas.*

Recently I spoke at a conference held in a remote area of Nebraska. My cabin was perched just below a train trestle, and what a special quality that place had because of the trains that rumbled through at all hours of the day and night.

I spent a great part of the night awake, but it was fun because I was fascinated with the first far-off toots of a train's whistle as it came to a crossing. Then I'd picture it as it would approach, pass by, and speed on through the night. As I listened closely, I learned to distinguish one kind of locomotive from another, just by the sound of the air horn or the clacking of the engine.

As I kept hearing the passing of the trains, I would reminisce about those times when I was a little girl visiting my aunt who lived where you could hear the trains go by in the night. What warmth there was in those familiar sounds!

The only train I hear these days is the steam locomotive at Knott's Berry Farm! How fortunate I felt that night to be able to listen through the night to those clacking sounds as the trains rumbled across the trestle high above my head.

On the way to breakfast the next morning, I looked up at the trestle and thought about how railroad tracks, themselves, are a work of art. In the early morning and late afternoon, as the sun moved toward the horizon, the tops of the rails shone with an almost radiant brightness. The highly polished steel stood out from the dull, weathered appearance of the ties and the ballast.

How beautiful these brightly glowing ribbons of steel appeared in the golden light of the sun. I couldn't help but make the connection that train tracks are beautiful only after taking tremendous weight, stress, and pressure, all of which polish them to their high luster. And the same is true of so many people I know.

As we ate breakfast, many of the women were complaining and some asked how I could sleep with all those train noises going on. I said I didn't mind, and then I asked one lady how come it seemed that all the trains were going east. Her reply, "Because that's the way the engine is headed!"

I refrained from reminding her that I was the one who was supposed be telling the jokes! Instead, I kept thinking how glad I was to be able to enjoy sounds and reminders of faraway times—finding joy in the small things. After all, I could always sleep at other places or at home, but seldom would I have the excitement of being awake most of the night listening to the passing trains and having my memories stirred so pleasantly.

Sounds do trigger my memories, and so do smells. Each of us can probably think of particular odors that are reminiscent of happy times. For those of us who live where the smell of burning leaves is still allowed by law, there are memories of high-school pep rallies and Halloween pumpkins. Or think about smelling dried pine needles and you're back in the woods on your first campout.

The scent of rubbing alcohol will probably always cause a twinge in the pit of your stomach as you remember childhood shots or hospital backrubs.

The sweet, old-fashioned perfume of purple lilacs evokes the ghosts of childhood backyards with brick walls and dense shade trees.

The smell of damp wool will always make me recall wet mittens with icy cuffs, snowballs, and apple-cheeked kids coming in out of the sub-zero cold.

Our ears and noses can teach us as much about life as any book. That's why I love to hear trains and whistles, as well as smell fresh-brewed coffee, baby powder, new leather, and gentle rain on summer dust.

And, personally, I love the smell of gasoline as it is being pumped into the tank. Maybe it reminds me of those long, cross-country car trips with the kids' Crayolas melting as we crossed the hot desert, eager to reach the next pit stop.

No matter what month of the year it might be, there are smells in the air that can trigger memories and make you feel alive. As J. H. Roades said:

> DO MORE THAN EXIST . . . LIVE!
> DO MORE THAN TOUCH . . . FEEL!
> DO MORE THAN LOOK . . . SEE!
> DO MORE THAN HEAR . . . LISTEN!
> DO MORE THAN TALK . . . SAY SOMETHING!

To this I would add: Do more than just smell a fragrance . . . *enjoy* it. In fact, enjoy everything you can while you can.

When I was growing up in Michigan, we bought apples by the barrel and my mother always made sure that we ate them ALL, even the mealy, soft, brown ones at the bottom. When I married Bill, I thought I had escaped having to eat mealy, brown, overripe fruit, but I quickly learned that he was just like my mom, only his specialty was bananas.

When the boys were small, Bill made sure that they ate ALL the bananas, even the ones that had gotten soft and speckled with brown. It seemed as though we never did get to eat nice, fresh, yellow bananas; we always were finishing up the brown ones—unless I tossed them out when Bill was at work! Maybe that's why I always love a new month, because I toss out everything leftover or overripe and start with fresh produce all over again. In my opinion, life is too short to eat brown bananas. And that goes for apples, too!

And although I'm glad I don't have to do that any more, I'm also glad Mom made us eat old, mushy apples and Bill made us eat the brown bananas. It taught me a valuable lesson that is found in one of my favorite readings, "The Station," by Robert J. Hastings. He definitely did not believe in eating brown bananas!

Tucked away in our subconscious minds is an idyllic vision in which we see ourselves on a long journey that spans an entire continent. We're traveling by train and, from the windows, we drink in the passing scenes of cars on nearby highways, of children waving at crossings, of cattle grazing in distant pastures, of smoke pouring from power plants, of row upon row of cotton and corn and wheat, of flatlands and valleys, of city skylines and village halls.

But uppermost in our minds is our final destination—for at a certain hour and on a given day, our train will finally pull into the station with bells ringing, flags waving, and bands playing. And once that day comes, so many wonderful dreams will come true. So restlessly, we pace the aisles and count the miles, peering ahead, waiting, waiting, waiting for the station.

"Yes, when we reach the station, that will be it!" we promise ourselves. "When we're eighteen . . . win that promotion . . . put the last kid through college . . . buy that 450 SL Mercedes Benz . . . pay off the mortgage . . . have a nest egg for retirement."

From that day on we will all live happily ever after.

Sooner or later, however, we must realize there is no station in this life, no one earthly place to arrive at once and for all. The journey is the joy. The station is an illusion—it constantly outdistances us. Yesterday's a memory, tomorrow's a dream. Yesterday belongs to a history, tomorrow belongs to God. Yesterday's a fading sunset, tomorrow's a faint sunrise. Only today is there light enough to love and live.

So, gently close the door on yesterday and throw the key away. It isn't the burdens of today that drive men mad, but rather the regret over yesterday and the fear of tomorrow.

"Relish the moment" is a good motto, especially when coupled with Psalm 118:24, "This is the day which the Lord hath made; we will rejoice and be glad in it."

So stop pacing the aisles and counting the miles. Instead, swim more rivers, climb more mountains, kiss more babies, count more stars. Laugh more and cry less. Go barefoot oftener. Eat more ice cream. Ride more merry-go-rounds. Watch more sunsets. Life must be lived as we go along.[1]

Robert Hastings is right. There is no station you can get to in this life that will make any difference, so you might as well enjoy the trip. But there is a very important Station that will come eventually.

While I was speaking in Canada, we came to the end of the conference and, because everyone would be leaving immediately after the final message, an announcement was made to put on your traveling apparel—they called it "going-home clothes." I couldn't help but think about that. We are all pilgrims making our trip homeward.

From years before, I remembered an old song we used to sing in "rounds." One side of the church would sing, "I'm on the homeward trail . . . I'm on the homeward trail . . ." and the other side would come back with "Singing, singing, everybody singing, HOMEWARD BOUND!" This would go on for several rounds, until the last strains of the song would be soft and almost distant, fading as the song ended with "HOMEWARD BOUND."

Through faith in Christ, we are all homeward bound. As God gradually transfers our loved ones to heaven, we have more and more deposits there, and as 1 Corinthians 2:9 says, "Eye has not seen, nor ear heard, nor have entered into the heart of man the things which God has prepared for those who love Him" (NKJV). What bright hope is in those words. And if ever there were a time when we needed hope, it is NOW!

Romans 15:13 says, "May the God of hope fill you with all joy and peace as you trust in Him, so that you may overflow with hope by the power of the Holy Spirit" (NIV). For me, overflowing with hope means overflowing with splashes of joy. So, if we don't get to splash joy down HERE, we'll splash joy together up THERE.

IN OUR FATHER'S HOUSE ARE MANY MANSIONS . . .
I HOPE YOURS IS NEXT TO MINE!

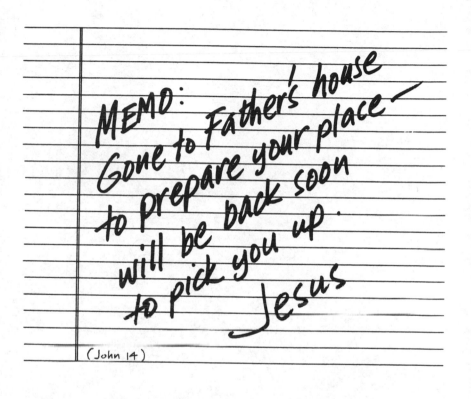

MEMO:
Gone to Father's house
to prepare your place —
will be back soon
to pick you up.
Jesus

(John 14)

# Endnotes

**Chapter 1 Smile! It Kills Time Between Disasters**

1. For one psychologist's viewpoint, see "It Pays to Be an Optimist Even When Almost Everyone Is Pessimistic," an interview with Dr. Martin E. P. Seligman of the University of Pennsylvania, *Bottom Line Personal*, 12, no. 10 (30 May 1991): 1.
2. Charles R. Swindoll, *Strengthening Your Grip* (Waco, Texas: Word Books, Inc., 1982). Used by permission.

**Chapter 2 How to Lay Down Your Agonies and Pick Up Your Credentials**

1. "Twelve Steps in the Grief Process," from Theos National Headquarters, 1301 Clark Building, 717 Liberty Avenue, Pittsburgh, Pennsylvania 15222.
2. Ida Fisher, *The Widow's Guide to Life* (Long Beach, Calif.: Lane Con Press), quoted in *Horizons*, a bimonthly newsletter published by Secure Horizons (July/August 1991), 1.
3. Edgar Guest, "To All Parents," from *All in a Lifetime*, originally published in 1938. Reprinted in 1970 by Books for Libraries Press, now an imprint of Ayer Company, Salem, New Hampshire. Used by permission.
4. Ann Landers, *The Ann Landers Encyclopedia, A to Z* (New York: Ballantine Books Edition, 1979), ix.

## Chapter 3 We Must Understand That It Is Not Always Necessary to Understand

1. Ashleigh Brilliant, *Pot-Shots*, No. 954, © Brilliant Enterprises, 1976. Used by permission.
2. The doctor's name was Benjamin Russ, and his book was *Medical Inquiries and Observations Upon the Diseases of the Mind* © 1836. It is quoted in Colin Murray Parkes, *Bereavement, Studies in Grief in Adult Life* (New York: International Studies Press, 1973).
3. See Ezekiel 11:19.

## Chapter 4 Wherever I Go, There I Am

1. Trina Paulus, quoted by Sue Monk Kidd, *When the Heart Waits* (New York: Harper & Row, 1990).
2. Josh McDowell, *Building Your Self-Image* (Wheaton, Ill.: Living Books, Tyndale House Publishers, Inc., 1988), 19, 20.
3. For more about these three "legs" of self-esteem, see Maurice Wagner, *The Sensation of Being Somebody* (Grand Rapids: Zondervan Publishing House, 1975), chapter 4. Wagner's book is an excellent discussion of how to build an adequate self-concept.
4. McDowell, *Building Your Self-Image*, 39–40.
5. Ashleigh Brilliant, *Pot-Shots*, No. 251, © Brilliant Enterprises, 1971.
6. Proverbs 12:25, TLB.

## Chapter 5 S.D.D.D.D. (Same Doo-Doo, Different Day)

1. Karol A. Jackowski, *Ten Fun Things to Do Before You Die.* (Notre Dame, Ind.: Ave Maria Press, 1989).
2. Janet Wagner's poem reprinted from Jackowski, *Ten Fun Things to Do Before You Die* (Notre Dame, Ind.: Ave Maria Press, 1989). Used by permission.

3. Adapted from "101 Ways to Cope with Stress," Life Focus Center, 2255 Broadway Drive, Hattiesburg, Mississippi 39402.
4. Ibid.
5. Poem by Ernest Lowe used by permission.
6. Ezekiel 36:25, NIV.

## Chapter 6 Laugh and the World Laughs with You . . . Cry and You Simply Get Wet

1. See Donald E. Demaray, *Laughter, Joy, and Healing* (Grand Rapids: Baker Book House, 1986), 25.
2. Norman Cousins, *Anatomy of an Illness as Perceived by the Patient* (New York: Norton, 1979) .
3. Dr. Laurence Peter and Bill Dana, *The Laughter Prescription* (New York: Ballantine Books, 1982), 8.
4. Peter and Dana, *The Laughter Prescription*, 9.
5. Demaray, *Laughter, Joy, and Healing*, 29.
6. See "A Laugh a Day May Help Keep the Doctor Away," *Prevention*, 43, no. 6 (April–May 1991), 50, 51.
7. From a message presented in 1989 by Marilyn Meberg, Lake Avenue Congregational Church, Pasadena, California. Used by permission.
8. Job 3:25, NKJV.
9. Leo Buscaglia, *Loving Each Other* (New York: Holt Rinehart and Winston, 1984), 116.
10. This story is included on one of the tape recordings of the late President Lyndon Johnson at the LBJ Presidential Library in Austin, Texas.
11. From an unidentified page entitled, "Mute Points and Other Figurines of Speeches." Its source is unknown.
12. The original source of this story is unknown. I have checked with three different newspaper/press associations in California and New York. All knew of the story and reported having seen it used in different settings, but none knew the actual source.

13. From a message presented in 1989 by Marilyn Meberg, Lake Avenue Congregational Church, Pasadena, California. Used by permission.
14. *Reminisce*, 1, no. 1 (1991), 46.
15. Ibid.
16. Ibid.

### Chapter 7 How Can I Be Over the Hill When I Never Even Got to the Top?

1. Remarkable Things, © 1988, Long Beach, California 90805. Used by permission.
2. I understand that Victor Buono died some years ago. I have no way of tracing the origin of this tape.
3. "Calories That Don't Count," Old Towne Press, 227 E. Chapman Avenue, Orange, California.
4. Anastasic Toufexis, "Forget About Losing Those Last Ten Pounds," *Time* (8 July 1991), 50.
5. Toufexis, *Time*, 51.
6. I am indebted to Ann Landers for some of these ideas on maturity.
7. Ashleigh Brilliant, *Pot-Shots*, No. 611, © Brilliant Enterprises. Used by permission.

### Chapter 8 Motherhood Is Not for Wimps

1. Original source unknown. Quoted in *Phyllis Diller's Housekeeping Hints* (New York: Doubleday & Company, 1966).
2. Remarkable Things, © 1988, Long Beach, California 90805. Used by permission.
3. From a column by Stan Walwer, "Why Mother's Tough to Understand," Highlander Newspapers, City of Industry, California. Used by permission.
4. Sondra Johnson, "Praying for Adult Children," reprinted with permission from *The Breakthrough Intercessor* © Breakthrough, Inc., Lincoln, Virginia 22078.
5. Ibid.

6. Original cross-stitch design by Pat Carson, Sumter, South Carolina. The poet is unknown.
7. L. J. Burke, quoted in "Promises for Parents: Daily reminders that children are a gift from God," A *DayBrightener* product from Garborg's Heart 'n' Home, Bloomington, Minnesota. Used by permission.

**Chapter 9 Oh, Lord, Let My Words Be Tender and Sweet for Tomorrow I May Have to Eat Them!**

1. Ashleigh Brilliant, *Pot-Shots*, No. 129, © Brilliant Enterprises, 1984. Used by permission.
2. Proverbs 13:12, TLB.
3. Proverbs 11:21, TLB.
4. Adapted from Toby Rice Drews, *Getting Them Sober*, vol. 1 (Plainfield, N.J.: Haven Books, 1980).
5. Psalm 30:5, KJV.
6. Barbara Johnson, *So, Stick a Geranium in Your Hat and Be Happy* (Dallas: Word Publishing, 1990), 167ff.
7. Proverbs 21:1, NKJV.
8. See James 1:19.
9. Adapted from Ken Durham, *Speaking from the Heart* (Fort Worth: Sweet Publishing, 1986), 99.
10. Ibid.
11. See Proverbs 16:24.

**Chapter 10 We Are Easter People Living in a Good Friday World**

1. From *Tell Me Again, Lord, I Forget,* by Ruth Harms Calkins (Wheaton, Ill.: © 1974). Used by permission of Tyndale House Publishers, Inc. All rights reserved.
2. "When I Come Home to Heaven," by Beth Stuckwisch © 1984. Used by permission of Dicksons, Inc., Seymour, Indiana.
3. Proverbs 12:25, TLB.

4. John 16:33, TLB.
5. Myra Brooks Welch, *The Touch of the Master's Hand*, (Elgin, Ill. : The Brethren Press, 1957).
6. See Barbara Johnson, *Fresh Elastic for Stretched-Out Moms* (Old Tappan, N. J.: Fleming H. Revell Co., 1986), 176–77.

**Encore! Encore! Going Up With a Splash**

1. Robert Hastings, "The Station," *A Penny's Worth of Minced Ham* (Carbondale, Ill., Southern Illinois University Press, 1986). Used by permission of Mr. Hastings.